Praise for *Dad's Book of Awe*

"I've got an eight-year-old who is going to love this book! Every project is manageable, not intimidating, and looks like so much fun. It's the perfect book of inspiration and ideas that we can refer to every time our daughter says, 'Let's make something!'"

> —Liesl Gibson, founder and designer of Oliver + S sewing patterns
> and author of *Oliver + S: Little Things to Sew*

"Any parent eager to raise a creative, can-do kid should be ready to hand over the tool box, the power drill, and this book. And then maybe run."

> —Lenore Skenazy, author of the book and blog *Free-Range Kids*

"*Dad's Book of Awesome Projects* is a pitch-perfect inspirational resource for creative projects to do with kids."

> —Whitney Moss and Heather Gibbs Flett, authors of *The Rookie Mom's Handbook*

"*Dad's Book of Awesome Projects* is that rare crafting book that is both hilarious and incredibly useful, whether you're looking to keep the kids busy for the afternoon or teach them the valuable lessons needed to leave you alone someday."

> —Stefanie Wilder-Taylor, author of *Sippy Cups Are Not for Chardonnay*
> and host of TV's *Parental Discretion*

"Finally, dads are getting the rad book of crafts we need and deserve."

> —Charlie Capen, co-creator of HowToBeADad.com and author of
> *The Guide to Baby Sleep Positions: Survival Tips for Co-Sleeping Parents*

DAD'S BOOK OF Awesome PROJECTS

From

STILTS AND SUPERHERO CAPES *to* TINKER BOARDS *and* SEESAWS

25+ FUN DO-IT-YOURSELF PROJECTS FOR FAMILIES

Mike Adamick

For Emmeline, my sidekick and inspiration,
and for Dana, who puts up with us.

Published by
Adams Media, a division of F+W Media, Inc.
57 Littlefield Street, Avon, MA 02322. U.S.A.
www.adamsmedia.com

ISBN 10: 1-4405-6119-2
ISBN 13: 978-1-4405-6119-1
eISBN 10: 1-4405-6120-6
eISBN 13: 978-1-4405-6120-7

Printed in the United States of America.

10   9   8   7   6   5   4   3   2

Photos by Mike Adamick and 123RF.com

This book is available at quantity discounts for bulk purchases.
For information, please call 1-800-289-0963.

CONTENTS

INTRODUCTION

If Martha Stewart and MacGyver ever hooked up and had a baby, it would look like this book.

While that would be enormously sad for the baby ("Oh, look at his cute duct tape?"), it is fortunate for you and your kids.

After spending years in the trenches of the home front—stay-at-home dad, classroom parent, PTA president, play-date planner, and playground pal—I learned that the most fun usually comes from those crazy, silly, makeshift games and inventions you come up with together on the fly.

That's the gist of this book.

You don't need to buy that expensive "crafting kit," that tool or appliance or cheap, lead-pocked plastic toy to forge memorable times with the kids. Whether you want to enjoy a rainy afternoon, spend a long, fun weekend together, or get your hands dirty with a bigger, longer project, you've probably got most of what you need in your pantry, your art bin, or maybe your storage area to have some seriously crazy fun times.

In a way, the philosophy behind this book offers a nostalgic throwback to the old school, hardscrabble childhoods of our grandparents and our parents—of our *own* childhoods, even. Not everything was available at the push of a button. Not everything came premade, shrouded in plastic. If you wanted to have a little fun, you had to make it yourself, using whatever parts you could find around the house.

So get ready to roll up your sleeves and work together. You never know what you'll create with a little duct tape, wood, glue, and gumption. But I can promise you this: You'll have the time of your lives.

How to Raise All-Around Crafty Geniuses. Or More Precisely . . . How to Use This Book

I'd like to say I grew up surrounded by crafts and woodworking, that I was raised on a steady diet of glue, grit, and ingenuity, that my childhood provided a kind of feral do-it-yourselfism drenched in a fantasyland of wood, drills, and the earthy aroma of sawdust.

Or that I have some sort of actual *training* when it comes to transforming the everyday detritus of life into something extraordinary for the home or for play time.

But I can't.

Here's the truth: I'm just some stay-at-home dad who became obsessed and overjoyed at the prospect of working with my daughter to make our own fun around the house. From planning play dates to organizing parties, from classroom parent duties to school PTA president responsibilities, I spent years assembling a bag of tricks and crafts for any moment. Over the years, I learned to master everything from the kitchen mixer to the sewing machine to the reciprocating saw.

Whether it's cooking our own Play-Doh, baking up cupcakes inside eggshells, or constructing our dining room table out of a banged up Victorian-era sliding door, I loved not just making things but spending so much quality time with my crafty sidekick.

When she was a toddler and we worked on projects together, Emmeline would hold nails or screws or would hand me the right tools at the right time. As she grew older and slightly more useful, she started measuring wood for cuts or, even later, wielding the saw or the drill. She loved to sit on my lap and push all the sewing machine buttons when we made superhero capes, costumes, or clothes. One summer she was suddenly old enough to attend Construction Camp and came home with wide eyes and stories about operating a chain saw and a chop saw.

"All on my own!"

She was six at the time.

We both beamed with pride.

Over the years, it seemed some of the best, most joyful times we had together came when we spent rainy afternoons or long weekends coming up with some crazy project to keep us busy: a cardboard boat for plying a deluged playground, a wooden catapult to knock over blocks, a '50s-era birdhouse for the backyard. We've built tables, bookshelves, hanging art installations, and paintings so pretty that people think we bought them at art fairs. We've made superhero capes out of old T-shirts, turned used books into Top Secret stashes, transformed leisure jackets into beautiful dresses, and turned worn shoes into something straight out of a comic book.

All without a workshop or a tool shed.

Instead of professional training or a garage full of tools, we relied on endless tinkering and crafting, on getting our hands dirty, on perseverance and doing our best with what was available. If something failed, we simply took it apart and tried again until we got it right.

The projects in this book represent what I learned in all my years on the home front. They are broken up into three main areas: crafts you can do in one afternoon, or sometimes even faster; crafts for a weekend; and crafts to work on during longer school breaks.

In using this book, I have four overarching tips to help you forge the best times together and to create some really amazing crafts.

Let Go

The projects in this book are all designed to be simple, fun projects you can do *together*—not just things *you* assemble while the kids sit idle on the sidelines, looking bored. Believe me, I've been there, done that, but these crafts are designed to bring you together and provide you with a guidebook for memorable moments.

If you suddenly find yourself with a lot of time on your hands and in need of a little extra fun, pull this book off the shelf and find a project you'd like to work on together. Some of the crafts you have to follow exactly, while others you can use as an inspirational resource to come up with something personal and special.

In using this book, please practice your best judgment about your child's capabilities. I don't mean that in the fear-mongering, legal sense, as in "For the love of god, *be careful!*"

No way. Quite the opposite, in fact.

That's where the term "Let go" comes into play.

Look, you know your kids better than anyone. When the time is right, don't be afraid to put the drill in her hand. Let him measure or hammer. Let her cut. Most of these projects are designed to let kids get their hands dirty right along with you. Some of the projects, like the swing or the seesaw, require more adult participation, but that's not to say the kids can't help with gathering supplies, measuring, drilling, or doing some installation work. In nearly all of these projects, the kids can, at the very least, take the leading role in design and decoration, using paint or colored duct tape to their hearts' delight. I've found that nothing makes a kid happier and prouder than the incredible sense of accomplishment of finishing a big project. This book aims to give you both those special moments, all while creating something useful and fun during the time you have together— whether it's an afternoon, a long weekend, or a summer break.

The point of all of this is to say: Whenever possible, let the kids take the lead. This may take a lot of time—a *lot* of time, believe me—and the finished product may not look like something out of Leonardo da Vinci's studio, but who cares? You should both just have fun working together. And the more the kids practice, the faster they will develop some incredible life skills. So let go. Back off a bit. And take your time.

Raise a Renaissance Kid

You will notice that some of these projects involve baking or cooking. Others involve sewing. Still more involve sawing or drilling. One delves into my personal fascination with the ol'-timey skill of whittling. There's no reason you shouldn't know how to do *all* of these things, and here's why: They all involve the same rule. Measure twice, cut once. The tools are just slightly different.

If you haven't gotten to know a sewing machine yet, you'll be surprised at how little sewing you actually do with one and how amazingly fun it is. If you're making, say, a flying shirt, most of the real work comes beforehand and involves measuring, cutting, ironing, and making sure everything is perfect and in order before you actually sew. In that way, a sewing machine is really no different from any other tool. You don't just grab some wood and a saw and then start cutting willy-nilly. You design, measure, prepare, and *then* cut, right? Same thing with sewing. I can't tell you how many jams I've gotten out of just knowing how to sew on a button or how to stitch up a pant cuff.

You may be a pro at the chain saw but know little about the oven. Conversely, you may know your way around a topstitch but are scared of a jigsaw. Well then, these projects are for you. From woodworking to painting, baking to gardening, there is a project in here for everyone, as well as opportunities to expand your crafty wheelhouse and to pass on that knowledge to the kids.

To that end, I'm only going to say this once— just so you don't have to keep hearing it in chapter after chapter—but while you're using all these awesome tools, please don't forget the proper safety gear: goggles, gloves, face masks, oven mitts, thimbles, shark suits—whatever you think is needed for a particular task. In fact, I don't list safety equipment at all under the "equipment" portions for each chapter, because I don't think you need reminding. Teaching tool safety should be your first lesson for each project, as you encounter more and more tools.

There.

Now that the After-School Special PSA is out of the way, let's move on to the third key tip in using this book.

Re-Use

Over the years, Emmeline and I have made scores, if not hundreds, of projects. In trying to pick which crafts to include in this book, I kept running across an underlying theme that really defines the time I want to spend with my child, and it's one I hope you will teach as well.

I discovered over the years that I was really a cheap skinflint at heart—more apt to create some ungodly dinner out of leftovers or to raid the pantry or freezer than to call for takeout. I used to make Emmeline's skirts and dresses out of fabric I cannibalized from thrift-store jackets and sheets.

That same philosophy applies to many of these projects. For some of them, you probably already have the necessary supplies on hand. For homemade ice cream, for instance, you need some plastic bags, some milk, and some ice— simple things, but you'll be surprised at how much fun this is. For wooden swords, I like to use old bed slats. For superhero capes or the flying shirt, any old T-shirt will do. You may have a cache of wood or crap in your junk drawer to make the perfect bicycle jump or a toddler tinker board. For the garden herb planter, you can get free wood while doing your regular grocery shopping. Seriously.

The point is, you don't have to run to the store to have a great time. As a parent trying to raise a responsible, resourceful child, I'm driven absolutely bonky by those craft-of-the-month boxes you can find on the Internet. Not all joy in life requires shopping—a lesson I think is particularly important to young girls constantly bombarded by pop culture advertising: "Buy this, buy that."

Some of these crafts require things you may not have around the house. One in particular, the swing set, actually advises you to buy a specific set of hardware. But for the most part, I'm saying take a moment to consider what you have on hand before clicking on Amazon. You'd be surprised at what you can breathe new life into.

Teach Grit

The last tip has to do with using these projects to teach the important art of gumption and grit, while also unplugging to enjoy your quality time together.

Remember MacGyver? From the television show in the late 1980s? He's the fictional hero for people who like to make stuff. But it goes beyond a silly punch line. You really *can* use everyday tools to work yourself out of difficult spots.

I'll always remember the afternoon when a package arrived at our house and we needed scissors to cut open the plastic. I asked for the tool and Emmeline instead tossed me a quarter. Poor child. My wife looked at her as if she would need extra special help at school. After all, couldn't she tell the difference between *scissors and coins?* I had forgotten altogether that I had already taught the kid this coin trick. I was proud as all get-out, as I started cutting through the plastic with the quarter.

There are myriad tiny lessons in personal resourcefulness that get lost in this age of all-consuming, instant gratification technology. It saddens me to see so many fellow parents just hand over a tiny screen for playtime and call it a day.

After all, if a child only taps on an iPhone all day, she'll never learn to defuse a bomb with a paper clip and some chewing gum.

I kid, I kid.

Sort of . . .

Look, I get it. I do. Screens are easy. And fun. We like to play iPhone games as much as the next family. But you can take these things a step beyond the screen and turn these passions into fun, quality time together—as opposed to sitting on the couch, staring at screens in silence, which seems to me as bad for the brain as for the body.

When my daughter learned about the *Angry Birds* video game, we played it for a bit but then created our own catapult out of closet dowels, a few scraps of wood, and some rubber bands. It took us all of one afternoon to make our own version of the game. Then we spent the next month building towers out of blocks and Lego bricks before knocking them down. We still enjoy playing the video game from time to time, but we have *way* more fun with our own real-life version of it.

Remember our own childhood, when Atari and ColecoVision were all the rage? We still managed to get out somehow and build bicycle ramps or make minnow traps or rope swings. And yet I all too frequently see kids who don't know the difference between a flat-head screwdriver and a Phillips head.

How did *that* happen?

I hope you'll use some of these projects to get your hands dirty, to teach lessons about tools, to unplug every now and then, to give the kids the expertise and experience they will need to get themselves out of jams, or to just relive the nostalgic crafts we once spent long afternoons working on with friends.

Mostly, however, I hope you'll use these crafts to have fun. That's really what these projects are all about.

AFTERNOON 1 CRAFTS

CIRCUS STILTS

"Stilts!" my daughter cried, rushing into the living room, "I need stilts!"

I didn't know she was even *aware* of stilts, let alone harbored frantic, half-panicked desires for them.

"And *why* do you *need* stilts?"

She looked at me as if I had just landed on the planet for the first time.

"Because I'm going to join the circus!"

Of course.

I once planned to run away and join the circus as well. Just substitute lion tamer or high-wire walker for stilt aficionado, and we share the same deep-seated circus dreams. (We also share the same paralyzing, soul-crushing fear of clowns, so even if she *does* join the circus, I'm confident she'll be back by nightfall.) It must be a phase. Every kid wants to join the circus at one point or another. So of course every kid needs stilts.

Luckily, stilts are ridiculously easy to create. You can make these in just a few hours, including all the measuring, cutting, drilling, cursing, recutting, and—my daughter's favorite—the duct-tape decorating.

Then you can spend the rest of the afternoon thinking about just how awesome it would have been to actually *join* the circus. Until you remember the clowns.

HERE'S WHAT YOU NEED

WOOD

❏ Two 2" × 2"s, and one scrap piece of 2" × 4" (We scored one for cheap in the scrap bin.)

BOLTS

❏ Two 3" bolts that look sturdy (don't go crazy; $5/16$"s worked for us), and two 5" bolts of same diameter (make sure they're all threaded the whole way)

❏ 4 washers

❏ 4 wing nuts (make sure they're the same diameter as the bolts)

DUCT TAPE

❏ Or paint, but then you have to wait for it to dry before you get to play with the stilts (And how tantalizingly horrible is that? To be done with a project and then wait to use it? No thanks.)

TOOLS

❏ Handsaw
❏ Drill
❏ Drill bit (same size as bolts)
❏ Sandpaper
❏ Measuring tape
❏ Pencil

HERE'S WHAT YOU DO

1 Saw the scrap 2" × 4" into an 8"-long chunk. Then cut it diagonally until you have two triangles.

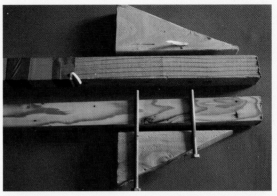

2 Place the triangles against the 2" × 2" so that they look like footrests. See how it works? *(See Fig. 1)* The thin part of the triangle points toward the bottom, and the thick part forms the footrest. *Boom.* You've got stilts. Well, almost.

Fig. 1

3 Drill two holes in each triangle—4" apart. Be precise.

4 Now switch to the 2" × 2" and start drilling holes, starting about 3" from the bottom. (See sidebar for tips.) Just keep going up, drilling a new hole every 4". Again, be precise. These holes should match up to the footrest holes as you adjust height. (You can drill as many holes as you like and who knows? Maybe your kid actually *will* join the circus. But take note of how high each new hole will make the footrest during later height adjustments, and just stop drilling where you feel comfortable.) *(See Fig. 2)*

Fig. 2

Fig. 3

5 Line up the footrest triangles to the holes in the 2" × 2"s and insert the bolts, washers, and wing nuts. You don't have to go bananas tightening them at first. Just make sure everything is lined up and mostly straight. *(See Fig. 3)*

6 Fit-test them for proper pole height. Circus clowns might have a precise measurement for how high the hand poles should be in relation to how high the footrests are placed, but we just eyeballed it and then cut the tops of the 2" × 2"s to a height my daughter felt comfortable with. Remember, as the kids get better, they may want to move the footrests higher, so make sure you leave enough of the 2" × 2" for future growth and then saw accordingly.

7 Decorate. Or not. We used colored duct tape because it's fun and easy and quick and lends a bright, circus feel to the whole project—plus it's something even a young kid can totally do on her own. But use whatever you like. Or don't. A nice smooth sanding on the wood is all you *really* need.

8 Start walking. Young kids will need a lot of balance help at first. It's almost like riding a bike: Once they get that balance right, they'll be walking all day.

DAD TIP

If your triangles turn out to be different sizes, don't worry. It's freaking hard to cut on the diagonal sometimes. But there's an easy fix. During Step 2, just place your triangle footrests on the 2" × 2"s and make sure the flat footpad parts—the tops—are even with each other. Then start drilling holes on the poles to make sure the footrests are always even with each other. It's not rocket science. Have fun. If you don't get everything right at first, figure it out. Even better, let the kid figure it out. If you really want, just skip the whole triangle business and turn the 2" × 4" into blocks, each about 6" long. This will give the stilts a chunkier look but could save on measuring and drilling time, especially if the triangles are different sizes. And honestly, kids don't care. They just want to walk on stilts. *Now!*

So there you go. You now have stilts.

Just think: For about $20 worth of materials, you just saved on *four* years of college. If, that is, the kid actually does go join the circus . . .

BALANCE BOARD

I'm always surprised at what a big hit it is when we make balance boards for friends. It's such a simple device—a board of wood and a cylindrical fulcrum underneath—but it contains some gravitational, almost magical pull of joy that is just too hard to resist.

When I'm working upstairs in our craft room, my daughter sometimes pulls out her old balance board and occupies herself for hours, trying to master the balancing act. Friends say their kids do the same. Heck, my wife and I pull it out every now and then and give it a try, long after the kid has gone to bed.

All told, it probably took us an hour to make and decorate our balance board, but it's the craft that keeps on giving.

SAFETY NOTE

This is potentially dangerous. I should tell you that from the start. The finished product will include sharp edges and the distinct possibility that you or your cherished loved ones will—gasp—fall.

Most likely on their rear ends.

Over and over again.

If you can get behind the idea that kids should live with a little danger mixed with a lot of fun, this is your project.

I kid you not: This is so much fun.

HERE'S WHAT YOU NEED

- ❏ Plank of wood (old fence, spare book shelf, used plywood, anything you can find)
- ❏ Strong cylinder (it can be wood, PVC pipe, whatever, so long as it's strong enough to support weight)
- ❏ Paint or duct tape or anything you want to decorate the board

TOOLS
- ❏ Handsaw
- ❏ Sandpaper

HERE'S WHAT YOU DO

1 Cut the plank until it's about the length of a skateboard, or even shorter. The shorter you make the plank, the more difficult it will be to balance, so start out long and work down from there after a few tests.

2 Cut the cylinder to match the width of your new board. You're going to be resting the board across the cylinder, creating the rolling fulcrum that makes this craft so awesome.

3 Test it out. Find the board length that works for you and the kids. You want it to be somewhat difficult to master, but not so difficult that it seems impossible. The goal is to stand on the balance board as long as possible with both edges of the board in the air at the same time. If you can do this right away for long periods of time, cut the board a little shorter and try again.

4 Once you're set on a good length, sand for smoothness and then decorate the plank and cylinder to your desires. I like to use colorful duct tape on the foot areas, but you can also paint it any color you want or even lacquer it up for an ol'-timey, polished feel. If you're giving one as a gift, customize it with a name or initials on the board. Then get balancing and have fun!

DAD TIP

I probably shouldn't have to tell you this, but then again, McDonald's probably never thought it had to tell people that coffee is, indeed, *hot*. Clear the area when you test out the board or start to play with it. Don't, for instance, test it in the same work area where your saw is. And remember, falls are likely. Also, don't use a toaster in the bathtub. You're welcome.

EGGSHELL CUPCAKES

Is there anything better than those long, slow, lazy fall afternoons when you have some free time to plop down and watch a game or maybe read a book?

Why yes. Yes there is.

Cupcakes.

But not just *any* cupcakes. Cupcakes baked in *eggshells*. And then injected with frosting, so that the best part is suddenly on the *inside*, appearing exactly like a yolk.

Now *that* is a pretty cool afternoon trick.

If you want to completely flip the kid's lid, or show up at school with some amazing birthday treats, or maybe kick up Easter-egg hunts a notch, this should be your go-to baking craft.

You don't have to be a fantastic baker. Maybe you'll use cake mix and one of those tins of waxy-tasting frosting for this. (Mmmm, wax.) It doesn't matter. You can use any recipe you want. You can get all fancy and use your favorite homemade cake and frosting recipe, or you can go the store-bought route and be done sooner. Up to you.

HERE'S WHAT YOU NEED

- ❏ Cake mix
- ❏ A dozen eggs (or more if you like)
- ❏ Muffin pan
- ❏ Tinfoil
- ❏ Plastic sandwich bag
- ❏ Frosting
- ❏ Baking syringe (housewares or craft stores sell these)
- ❏ Vegetable oil or oil spray
- ❏ Optional: Egg dye and crayons for decoration

HERE'S WHAT YOU DO

1 While your kitchen helper makes the cake batter, prepare the eggs. It's easy. Over a bowl, simply punch a hole in the bottom with a knife point or anything sharp and punchy. Then use your fingers to open up a quarter-sized hole or so. Dump the egg whites and yolks in a bowl, and then rinse out the shells. Some of your eggs can be used for the cake mix, and the rest can be saved for dinner.

DAD TIP

I like to do this project in the afternoon or very early in the morning, because there's a lot of leftover egg. Make an omelet or a dinner frittata if you don't want to waste all those extra yolks.

2 When the eggs are all hollowed out, prepare the muffin pan by making little nests out of tinfoil. They don't have to be perfect and there's no one right way to do it—just make sure the eggs can stand up straight for baking and you're good to go. This is a perfect job for your helper. *(See Fig. 1)*

3 Now, spray the inside of the eggs with oil or pour a dab in and swirl it around to coat. This is key to prevent sticking when you're later peeling the eggs to get at the cupcakes. Shake out any excess oil just before filling the shell with batter.

4 Pour some cake batter into a sandwich bag to make your own pastry bag. Cut a hole in the corner of the bag and then squeeze the batter into the egg holes. Fill them no more than three-quarters or they will ooze during baking. (They'll probably ooze anyway, but you can cut down on this by filling carefully.)

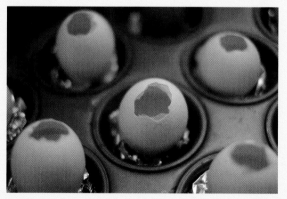

Fig. 1

5 Bake away. The time really depends on the recipe, your oven, how full the eggs are, etc., etc., etc. Try 15 minutes at first and then test them with a toothpick. It should come out clean. If not, bake a little longer until ready.

6 Now, the *really* fun part. When the eggs are done and cooled a little bit, break out the frosting. Either buy yellow frosting or tint your own with food coloring.

7 It's syringe time! This part is so much fun. You can usually get syringes at an art supply store or a kitchen wares store. Now, stuff the syringe with frosting and then poke it through the egg hole and into the cake. Fill the cake eggs with as much as you think they'll hold without bursting. This part is not tricky, just messy. Let the kids do this because otherwise *you'll* get a sugar high from licking your fingers so often.

8 Clean off any excess cake ooze. No matter what you do, the cake may ooze out of the egg. No big deal. Use a sharp knife to scrape the ooze away and then a wet paper towel to clean it all off. Voilà! Your eggs are ready to go. Enjoy the coolest-looking cupcake you will ever eat in your *life*.

DAD TIP

For special events you can dye the eggs beforehand. Or you can simply use crayons to decorate them when you're done baking. If you really want to have fun, toss one gently to a friend or spouse, being sure to conceal the hole. They'll momentarily think (a) they're doomed to a raw egg mess and (b) that you've lost your mind. Until they realize, of course, that you just tossed them a cupcake and that you're the Best. Person. In the *world!*

COMIC BOOK SHOES

I miss Saturday mornings.

Remember when you used to creep downstairs while your parents remained in bed? Your siblings would already be up, parked in front of the TV, luxuriating in the warm glow of pixelated bliss. You'd get your own cereal and heap loads of sugar onto flakes that were probably frosted enough as is. Afterward, you'd tilt the bowls and savor the gooey remains of so much sugar milk.

It was pure heaven.

Bugs Bunny. Hanna-Barbera. The Saturday morning cartoon marathons were a treat; nothing like what kids today experience with their twenty-four-hour access to OnDemand or an iPad's instantaneous satisfaction.

It was our time. Kid time. No school. No homework. Nothing to do but vegetate.

Over the years, one thing remains the same, however, no matter if you're watching cartoons on your laptop or if you're still waiting for Saturday mornings. Everyone loves superheroes.

If you really want to brighten the world of someone young at heart, this is the superhero project for you. And who knows? You might just find an old pair of shoes of your own in need of a good makeover.

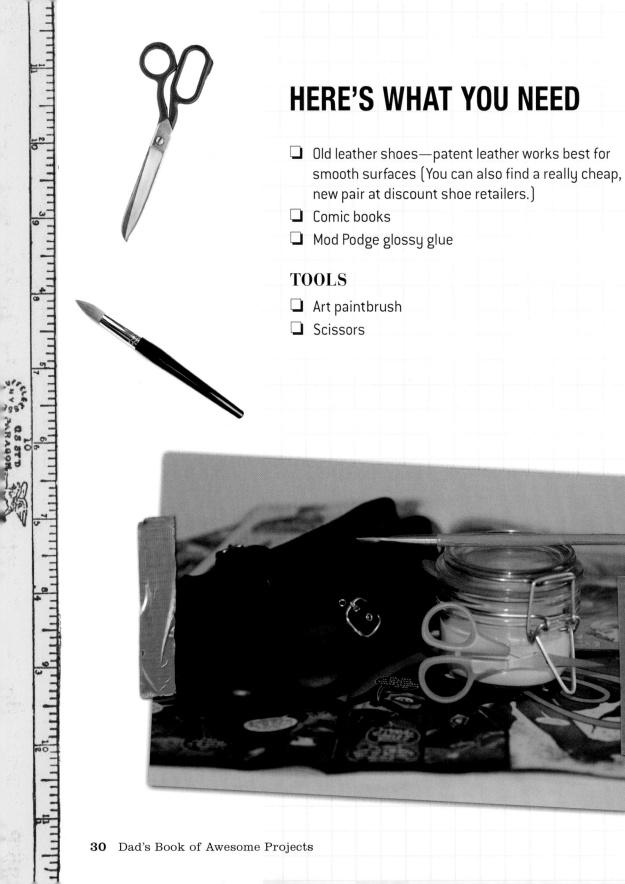

HERE'S WHAT YOU NEED

- ❑ Old leather shoes—patent leather works best for smooth surfaces (You can also find a really cheap, new pair at discount shoe retailers.)
- ❑ Comic books
- ❑ Mod Podge glossy glue

TOOLS

- ❑ Art paintbrush
- ❑ Scissors

HERE'S WHAT YOU DO

1 Round up your favorite comic books. Hmm, let me take that back. Maybe not your *favorite*. That first edition Superman could make for some pretty cool albeit ridiculously pricey kids' shoes. Scratch that. Round up some unwanted comic books and start cutting. Cut out small characters, cool drawings, all the POW!s and KaBLAM!s and whatever else you want. I'm particularly fond of inserting non sequiturs, like a dialogue bubble that says, "Ow! My arm!" or "Thankfully I'm not melting in the firewalls." In the books, in context, they make sense. On the shoes, they are a riot. The point is, cut out a lot of snippets and words and small characters that won't get lost or won't, conversely, take over (looking at you, Wolverine). Make sure a lot of them have straight bottoms or straight tops. You'll need these to glue on where the shoe leather meets the soles.

2 Once you have a sufficient amount of pieces, large and small, start sort of mapping them out on the shoe. You don't have to be precise; just make sure that really cool cut-out of Spiderman, say, will work on the toe or the heel or the side— wherever. Once you have a rough plan in mind, you can go to the next step. But if you find you need more pieces, keep cutting until satisfied. Kids love to cut out the pieces.

3 Glue on the pieces with Mod Podge. I like to put a light coat on the shoe thin enough to get tacky quickly. Place the cut-out pieces on the leather, starting at the edge of the sole, using pieces that have flat bottoms. Go around the whole thing. Now, go around the tops of the shoes with pieces that have flat tops. When finished, you should have an uneven band of visible leather between the top and bottom. Start filling that in with pieces. I like to save larger pieces for this; action pieces with Wonder Woman or Superman kicking ass work exceptionally well.

4 Don't be afraid to get messy. You can use your fingers to smooth pieces out or hold them in place. Don't worry if some of the paper bends or folds. Just add more Mod Podge and all your problems will be solved. The glue will help soften the paper for bends and help keep it down as well. A few seconds of firm pressing seems to keep bendy pieces in place.

5 Once you've slathered up the shoe and filled up every spare inch with comics, lightly brush the whole shoe with a coat of Mod Podge. Then, wait an hour or so and do it again. It will make sure everything stays on just right and you'll get a high-gloss sheen that looks professional.

 6 Go find your own shoes and repeat.

DAD TIP

Don't be afraid to overlap pieces. If you need to fill a gap, just add some more Mod Podge and cut out a piece to fit. You'll notice that by the second shoe, you're a real pro at this. This project was so much fun and so easy that we started making them as gifts for friends.

VINTAGE MODERN SILHOUETTE

We have a tradition of making gifts for important occasions, as opposed to buying some forgettable item from the store.

We're obnoxious, elitist snobs that way, I know . . .

I kid. We're just ungodly cheap.

The point is, it's nice to get something that you know took a loved one a long, painful time to make.

One of my favorite items in the whole world is the coffee mug my daughter made for Father's Day. She and my wife went to a paint-it-yourself pottery studio and decorated this mug just for me. I love it so much that, weirdly, I rarely drink from it, as I'm so scared of accidentally breaking it. Crazy, I know. But I don't want to see anything happen to it.

For our eighth wedding anniversary, my wife, Dana, crafted a button-down linen shirt for me because according to tradition, linen fabric was that year's "anniversary gift." She even created a special tag for it from one of our wedding photos. This has become one of my favorite articles of clothing—so much so that people are probably beginning to think I own only one shirt.

One year, as Mother's Day approached, I was trying to come up with something special for Dana when I spotted one of those neat Victorian necklaces featuring a silhouette at a consignment shop. You've probably seen these. They sport a pearly outline of big-haired women against a black backdrop. Inspiration and memories immediately collided, as I recalled the silhouettes my mom had made of us three boys—outlines of our faces in black, done against a nice Victorian-looking backdrop.

What if I made a silhouette of our daughter, but fancied it up a touch—gave it a modern flair? Something that we'd be proud to display anywhere in the house?

All in all, this craft takes about an hour—from printing a photo to cutting a stencil to spray-painting the scene. But it makes for an incredible, personalized gift you'll all cherish forever. In fact, it would be cool to make a new one each year to trace a child's growth.

HERE'S WHAT YOU NEED

- ❏ Display surface—A wood block or canvas will do nicely.
- ❏ Spray paint—one bright color of your choice, and one plain white.
- ❏ A photo—Basically any photo will do, provided the kid is turned sideways with a perfect profile.
- ❏ Stencil paper—You can find the plastic-y stuff at your favorite craft store. Clear file folders will work in a pinch.

TOOLS

- ❏ X-Acto knife or craft knife of choice to cut stencil
- ❏ Scotch tape

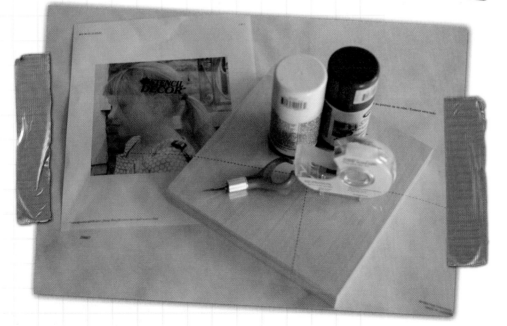

HERE'S WHAT YOU DO

1 Paint the surface you're going to put the silhouette on. You can use a nice block of wood for the surface with a light coat of spray paint on it—enough to color the wood and give it pop but not enough to overwhelm it and get rid of all the neat grain. You can also use a canvas to fit into a frame. Up to you.

2 As you're waiting for the surface paint to dry, get to work on finding a photo that shows your child in perfect profile. You might want to pay attention to the hair as well. For instance, photos of girls in ponytails or pigtails work much better than down hair, which can look blobby in a silhouette. Boys with a little cowlick or stray locks up front work great as well. It doesn't matter what your photo is printed on—photo paper or just plain office paper—as you're only using it as a tracing guide and you'll be cutting it up soon. But make sure it's big enough to provide the size silhouette you want. Enlarge it on the printer if needed.

3 Take your stencil paper and lay it on top of your photo. Tape it down if you can. Now, use your knife to cut out the outline of your silhouette. You should really, really take your time with this step and do the best you can, following the nose, eyes, lips, chin, and face perfectly. If you don't get it right the first time, try again. It's worth it to make it right.

4 Now you have a stencil sheet with a child-shaped hole in it. *(See Fig. 1)* Perfect. Nice work. When your wood block or canvas is dry, center the stencil silhouette over where you want to paint the silhouette. The stencil should cover your whole surface, with just the child-shaped hole available to paint through. If any of the colored surface is still exposed, cover it with newspaper so as not to get white paint on it. Make sure your stencil is secure and is not going to slip. You can press it down with your fingers until you're happy with it.

Fig. 1

Once you're ready, spray on a light dusting of white paint. Whatever you do, don't hold the can too close to your surface. Start about 10" away and add a light layer. If you want to make it a little darker, dust it up a little more—tiny bits at a time. This will prevent you from adding so much paint that it pools up and begins to leak under the stencil, turning your silhouette into a blobby, drippy mess. Take it slow. You don't really need much anyway, as the white paint will show up beautifully against the colored surface.

DAD TIP

Keep the stencil! You can use it again and again on different colored surfaces for a tremendous home art installation or as a child's room decor! And remember the head-shaped stencil you cut out? Try putting that on a colored block of wood and then adding white spray paint around it for a different look.

Once you feel comfortable with the paint coating, remove your stencil and *boom!* you're done. Let the wood block dry then hang it up or prop it on a desk. Same goes if you used a canvas. Once dry, just insert it into your frame of choice and get wrapping. I hate to keep saying that all these crafts are super easy and simple, but really, they are. The hardest part of this one is cutting out the stencil, but only because you have to be super precise. The rest is just adding light coats of paint. How difficult is that?

CRAYON SHAPES

If you've got a child old enough to draw, you probably have this problem: crayon nibs. Busted, broken bits of crayon. A piece here. A chunk there. A stray crayon nestled among the couch cushions. How on earth did one get in the *freezer*?

We all like to keep track of our art supplies and secure them in an art bin, but crayons, I've determined, are sentient. They are living, thinking, tricky little buggers who apparently have lived in a box long enough. Give them just one inch of daylight and poof . . . they're gone.

I try to corral them when I see them on the run, stuffing them back into the box or putting them into Mason jars, the kryptonite of all runaway crayons (well, not really, but it makes me feel better to think I just got one over on a child's coloring implement).

All of this is to say: You probably have a lot of stray crayon bits around your house or floating around your art bin.

This is the perfect way to do something incredibly cool with them.

HERE'S WHAT YOU NEED

- ❏ Crayon nibs . . . crayon bits . . . piles and piles of broken, busted runaway crayons
- ❏ A muffin pan

TOOLS

- ❏ X-Acto knife
- ❏ Small cookie cutters (small enough to fit into muffin molds—and any shape of your desire)
- ❏ Oven

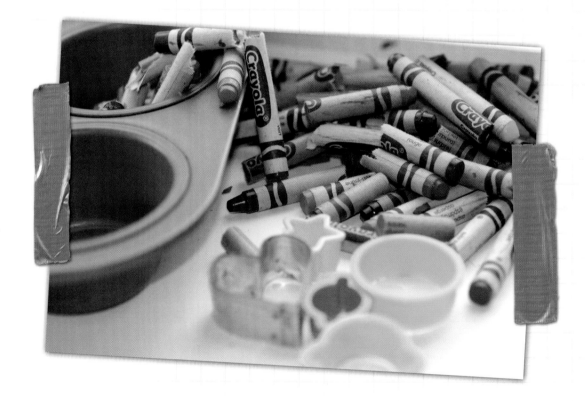

HERE'S WHAT YOU DO

1 Preheat the oven to 250°F. You don't have to bake these little guys into oblivion—just enough to melt them down.

2 Peel off all the paper wrappings on your stray crayons. A slit with an X-Acto knife will save your fingernails from billions of wax shavings jammed deep down, the crafting equivalent of waterboarding.

3 Break apart crayons into tiny, centimeter-long chunks (no need to be exact here) and then fill muffin tins about halfway up with small piles of the chunks. *(See Fig. 1)* You don't have to be precise on the size, but keep an eye on the colors. Make sure you add powerful, glowing bits of color to otherwise drab piles. In other words, if you see you have a lot of blues and purples, add a nib of white or orange. It adds a dash of brightness to each batch. Or not. Up to you. All red or all blue would also work quite well. I just like the rainbow effect.

4 Bake for about 5 to 8 minutes and check. If the wax is completely melted, take the tin out and let it cool. If not, bake it for another couple minutes and keep checking. The finished product should resemble a soup made by Oompa Loompas.

5 When all the wax is melted, take it out and let it cool. Now here comes the tricky part. You can't wedge the cookie cutters in too soon or the soup won't hold its shape. And you can't wait tooooo long or the soup will harden and you won't even get the cookie cutters in. After about five minutes, poke around the soup. It should be congealing nicely. When ready, push in the cookie cutters (small ones that fit in the muffin tin, obviously) and just leave them. Now wait for everything to harden.

Fig. 1

6 Once the soup has hardened—give it a good half hour at least—take a butter knife or small spatula and go around the edges of the muffin tins. A whole disk should pop out of each tin, with the cookie cutter still wedged inside. Punch the new crayon shape formed by the cookie cutter gently out of the disk. Voilà! You have a cool new rainbow-colored crayon. You also have a neat cut-out disk of crayon to either play around with or remelt to make even more shapes. Enjoy!

DAD TIP

This is potentially dangerous, so test it yourself first: While the crayon soup is cooling, dip all your fingertips into it. *Only do this when the temperature is low enough not to burn you.* The wax should just coat your fingerprints, and then you have "Crayon Hands" to make some neat drawings. The wax tends to break apart pretty easily once it's on your fingers, but come on, how can you pass up the opportunity for Crayon Hands?

DUCT TAPE CRAYON WALLET

When it comes to family meals at our house, we have a hard-and-fast rule: no electronics.

Let's face it; that e-mail can probably wait fifteen lousy minutes without the world exploding or giving the terrorists a win.

Look, I'm not anti-technology, not some Luddite yammering on against modernity. But something about screen time during meals drives me bonkers. I don't like to inhabit one world while my companions are off in another, virtual world. That can't be good for quality family time.

So how do we handle dining out with kids?

Crayons.

Good ol'-fashioned hardened wax.

Using scraps of leftover fabric and a little duct tape, the kid and I spent an afternoon crafting up our own personal crayon-and-paper wallet—something she can carry to restaurants to keep busy during longer meals. She's happy to draw or color, and the whole family is sometimes drawn into games of hangman or tic-tac-toe while waiting for food. That has to be better than the hottest app of the moment, right?

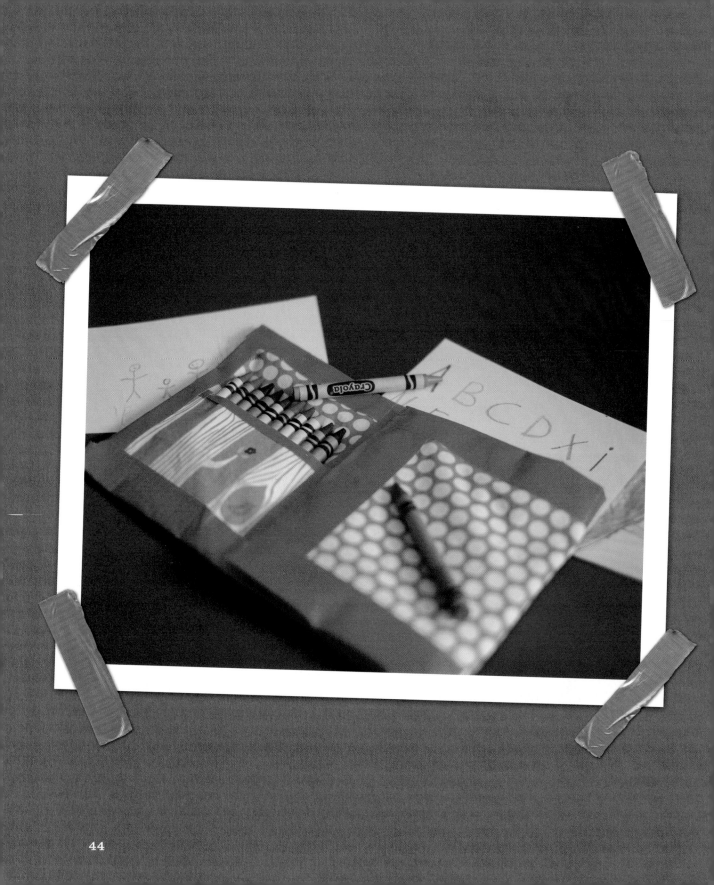

HERE'S WHAT YOU NEED

- ❏ Your favorite scraps of fabric: 2 same-sized rectangles approximately 6" wide by 12" long and 1 strip 3" wide by 12" long
- ❏ Duct tape
- ❏ Crayons, index cards, or paper scraps

TOOLS

- ❏ Scissors
- ❏ An iron

HERE'S WHAT YOU DO

1 Iron all your fabric and make it nice and smooth and flat. Easy peasy. You don't need much. Two pieces of fabric should look like a rectangle—approximately 6" wide by 12" long. One strip of fabric should be the same length but only 3" wide—basically a long strip. This is the piece that will hold the crayons and paper in the wallet.

2 Lay out the long, thin strip first. Cut or tear some duct tape about the same length as the strip and seal it to the top, long edge of the fabric, sealing both sides of the edge in tape. Make it nice and smooth. This will form the crayon-and-paper pouch. *(See Fig. 1)*

DAD TIP

Here's a quickie lesson on fabric terms, as you'll need to know them for the next few steps. See that bright, colorful side where the pattern is? The part that you wear on the outside? That's called the "right side." The other side, the part that goes against your body, is called the "wrong side." I don't know why it's not called the inside or the outside. But whatever. That's what all the clothes patterns call them.

As for fabric selection, it doesn't really matter. Choose whatever you like or let the kid do it. If you don't have fabric scraps taking up space, cut up an old shirt—not one made of T-shirt material but an old button-down shirt.

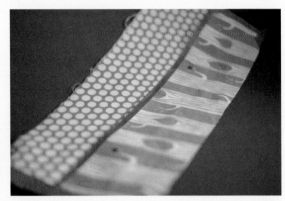

Fig. 1

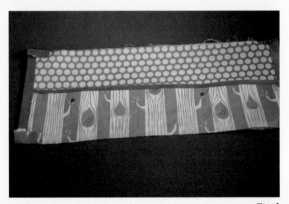

Fig. 2

3 Now take the two bigger rectangles and lay them on top of each other so that the wrong sides are touching. In other words, you should see the pattern on the outside of both pieces. Make sure everything is lined up. Lay that long strip you have already duct-taped so that the bottom of your strip matches up to the bottom of your rectangles. The duct-taped top portion of your strip should cut across the middle of your rectangle from side to side. *(See Fig. 2)*

4 Tear off some thin pieces of duct tape—about ½" wide—and run them from the bottom of the wallet to the top to form folders for crayons and paper. It doesn't matter if you go over the top of the fabric a little bit. You'll be sealing all the sides with duct tape soon enough. The point of this is to form little dividers for crayons and paper. Use three or four strips across the wallet, or even more if you like.

5 Once you're satisfied with your pockets, seal the side edges of your rectangles with duct tape. Just tear off a regular strip of duct tape about the same width as your wallet and then place the wallet on top of the strip. Fold and seal. Make it nice and smooth. Repeat this process for the longer sides. Make sure everything is smooth and looks pretty.

DAD TIP

I've found that the duct tape works surprisingly well on fabric. Just make sure you press it down hard and seal it. If you have to redo parts, it's really no biggie. Take your time and make sure everything is smooth and will hold. If you're nervous, feel free to use staples to reinforce your pocket dividers. Or use a sewing machine to stitch in dividers instead of duct tape.

6 Find your favorite crayons and some scrap paper and stuff them into the pockets. You're good to go. You now have your own portable crayon-and-paper wallet.

FRIENDSHIP BRACELETS

It doesn't matter if you have a boy, a girl, or just a really cool relative you baby-sit every now and then. Kids. Love. Friendship bracelets. You should have this craft in your pocket, ready to pull out at a moment's notice.

Many kids collect them and trade them. Like the circus thing, it must be a phase kids go through. At some point, their wrists are going to be adorned with so much thread and rope, you'll start to wonder which dock they plan to moor themselves to.

Don't question it. Just go with it.

The really sweet thing about friendship bracelets is how easy they are to make. You don't need much—just some string thicker than regular sewing thread. Embroidery thread works perfectly and is, in fact, the stuff you'll find in those rip-off "Friendship Bracelet Making Kits." I say rip-off because let's face it: Those kits cost ten to twenty bucks, but a whole package of embroidery thread costs a fraction of that.

Just buy the thread and you're good to go.

Now, there are tons of different kinds of friendship bracelets you can make, but here's a very simple one you can pull out of your bag of tricks at any moment: the Chinese Staircase. (The bonus of this one is that it puts you in a stress-reducing, meditative zone—more on that later.)

When the kids master this, you can move on to chevrons and eight-layer braids and whatever else you want. But this is a good starting point and so easy and fun that soon you'll be making whole messes of them.

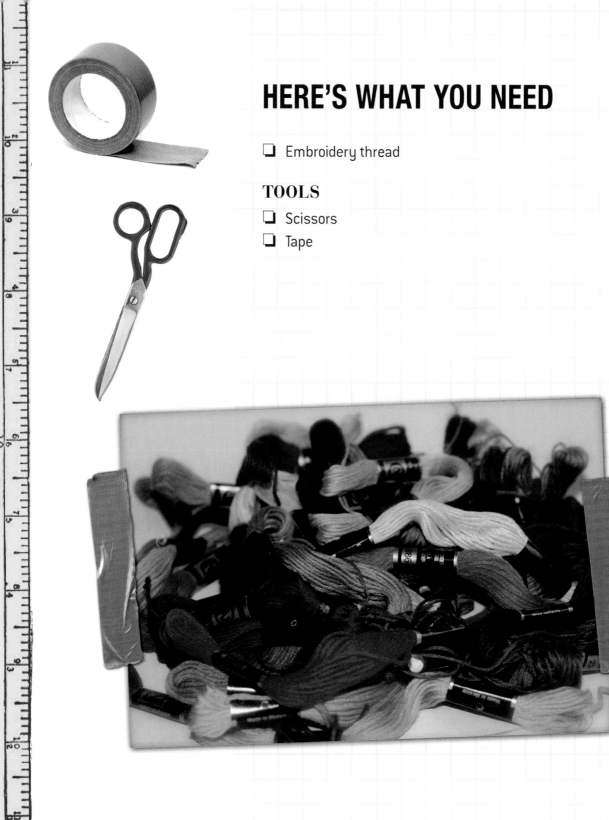

HERE'S WHAT YOU NEED

❑ Embroidery thread

TOOLS
❑ Scissors
❑ Tape

HERE'S WHAT YOU DO

1 Select your colors—three, tops. You may be surprised by the inglorious clash of colors your child selects; personally, I would have never thought of pairing up green with pink and black, but you know, it sort of worked, so just go with it. Yes, you may be asked to wear this bracelet later, and how will you be able to say no to your proud child? Well, you can't.

2 Measure out each colored thread from the tips of your fingers to your elbow and cut it so you have three similar-sized pieces.

3 Take all your colors, line them up so the ends are even, and tie a knot in one end. Leave about an inch or so after the knot. You'll use this part to tie the bracelet around a wrist later.

4 Find a place that's comfortable because you'll be there for a while. No, I mean it. Find a really comfy place. Trust me. Tape that knot to your work surface—a table, a book, even your knee if you want to sit down and use your lap as your work surface. Soon, you'll be in a meditative knot-tying zone you didn't even know existed and you'll feel all your stress and worry just melt away. So get comfy and enjoy the side effects of friendship bracelets: major stress relief. (Remember how awesome it was to be a kid with few responsibilities and summer breaks? It'll come back to you with this craft, promise.)

5 Ahhhh. Okay. Ready? Draw one color from the other two at an angle. Now, fold that one color back over the other two. You should now have what looks like a 4. See how that one line in the 4 goes off and forms a triangle and then goes back and goes over the straight line? That's what one of your threads should do. *(See Fig. 1)*

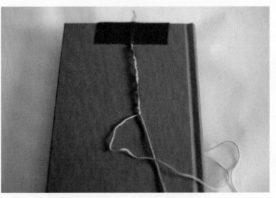

Fig. 1

Loop the one color under the other two and back over them. Pull gently until you have a knot. Make sure you hold on to both pieces of thread—the one color you're using to loop and the two colors you're looping around. Pull gently until you form a knot at the top of your thread.

 Now, repeat. A lot. Like, ten times. Stick with one color until your bracelet starts to develop a band of that one color. Then, when you feel like you've had enough—ten times usually does it—switch to the next color and watch as another band of color develops.

8 When the bracelet starts to take shape and seems long enough, try to wrap it around the wrist that will be wearing it. If it's not yet long enough or just what you want, keep looping and making more bands of color. Then retest it for wearing. Once you're happy, tie a knot in the end that's not taped down and tie the whole thing around the wearer's wrist, cutting off any excess. Wasn't that easy? Fun? Awesome? Well, be warned: You may be making a lot of these once you master it.

HOMEMADE PLAY-DOH

I love everything about Play-Doh . . . except the smell. To me, it smells awful—a freak show of aroma straight out of a hygiene nightmare. And this from a guy who doesn't believe in hand sanitizers.

But is it ever *fun*. It's the perfect afternoon timesuck—a craft that keeps on giving because you can always squish your creation and start again.

When I was a kid, I was amazed to walk into a friend's house and see his mom hunched over the stove, cooking up what appeared to be a giant vat of green mashed potatoes. How cool, I remember thinking. Green potatoes!

When I finally realized it wasn't food—what? I was a slow child—life was never the same again.

It was as if she had just discovered the god particle, right there in the 'burbs. "You mean you can make your *own*?"

Kids seem equally as impressed today as I was back then. Here's why: Making your own Play-Doh is almost as fun as actually playing with it.

It's cheap, for one. It only takes a few minutes and you probably already have the ingredients you need. Plus, you can customize it any way you want—adding a pinch of color here or a dash of food flavoring there for better smell. Nothing beats regular Play-Doh like vanilla-scented play-dough.

Mmmm, you can almost eat it—except for the whole tastes-like-a-salt-lick thing . . .

Here's a simple recipe for rainy days or play dates.

HERE'S WHAT YOU NEED

- ❏ 2 cups flour
- ❏ 1 cup salt
- ❏ 2 cups water
- ❏ 2 tablespoons vegetable oil
- ❏ 1 tablespoon cream of tartar
- ❏ Food coloring
- ❏ Food flavorings or scented oil for smell (optional)

HERE'S WHAT YOU DO

1 Mix everything except the food coloring and flavoring or scented oils in a saucepan. Let the kids do this. It ain't rocket science. If they spill a little, who cares? Just make like the Brawny Man and wipe that mess up.

2 Now cook it over low heat, stirring every now and then. When it starts caking to the bottom, you're almost there. Just keep stirring, making sure the heat is low enough not to burn it. You'll eventually notice it lumps up quite nicely and becomes less sticky and more . . . tacky. You'll know it when you see it.

3 When it's done, plop the ball onto the counter or a chopping block. After it cools to a touchable temperature, start kneading. It can get surprisingly warm—it shouldn't really be hot—and mmmm, it can feel sort of good. After some kneading, it will *really* begin to resemble Play-Doh—all smooth and perfect. Almost done.

4 If you want to improve the aroma, add the scented oil or flavoring and knead in. This stuff already smells way better than the carnival of funk that comes out of a store-bought Play-Doh can.

5 Divide the dough into as many pieces as you have color for. This is the cool part. If you want a lot of red, break off a big hunk. If you just want a little green, break off a tiny piece. You're in control.

DAD TIP

This is one of those crafts that will almost feel like a letdown. I'm sorry. But after making this for the first time, you'll probably do what I did: shake your head and say, "That's it? *Seriously*?"

Because yes, it's *that* easy.

Fig. 1

Add food color to all your pieces and knead the dough until the color is mixed evenly and you're satisfied with the brightness. *(See Fig. 1)* Again, this is all stuff the kids can do while you sit back with a cup of coffee and "supervise." (My supervision of this craft now usually involves reading the newspaper.)

When you're all done playing with the stuff, just store the pieces in a sealed sandwich bag or whatever food containers you have lying around. If stored correctly, it lasts for a whole mess of months and doesn't leave you feeling all icky like regular Play-Doh.

GARDEN TROLLEY

We have a small backyard, with a square-shaped patch of grass in the middle ringed by flower beds, some bushes, and a leafy fig tree. It may be a small yard, but it's great to have a place to go climb a tree or dig in the dirt or plant flowers and herbs.

One of the best, most useful things we ever did for our backyard adventures was to create a simple garden trolley. I got the idea from my father-in-law, who is constantly tinkering around his house. One day, he built a trolley to carry things around easily, and I replicated that for our own yard.

I use it to haul soil for planting or to bring in beds of flowers or heavy tools—whatever the project of the day is. During play time, the kid likes to load it up with hand shovels and flowerpots to create her own projects. Or, sometimes, she puts some toys on it for a makeshift hayride.

One day I was doing the dishes and getting ready for dinner when I couldn't find her. I checked the backyard and there she was, loading and unloading toys from the trolley, letting her toys take turns on the "ride." She did this for about an hour, at which point I labeled this the Best. Craft. Ever.

HERE'S WHAT YOU NEED

❏ A plank of wood—I used an old shelf from an abandoned bookcase.

❏ Casters and screws (usually pretty cheap for a set of four)

❏ A rope—3' or 4'

❏ Paint, duct tape, stain, whatever you want to decorate

TOOLS

❏ Saw

❏ Drill

HERE'S WHAT YOU DO

1 Cut the wood into a good-sized rectangle. It doesn't have to be any particular measurement, just something you think is big enough to haul stuff around on or do the job you want it to do.

2 Install one caster on each corner, being careful to make sure the screws are long enough to go into the wood but not too long—otherwise they pop through the wood and create sharp spikes where you will be loading things or giving the kid a ride. *(See Fig. 1)*

3 Drill a hole on one end of the trolley and insert rope, tying it to the trolley. Voilà. Done.

DAD TIP

If your screws are a bit long, add small blocks of wood on the top side. When you install the casters, the screws will go through the trolley wood and then stick into the wood blocks. *Boom!* Now you've got little handles for the kiddos and you've managed to hide pesky, painful screws. Chalk that one up in the "win" column.

It doesn't really take longer than a half hour to make this. Just screw on casters, add a rope, and you're ready to go. If you'd like, feel free to decorate it any way you want—paint, duct tape, a nice stain finish. *(See Fig. 2)* Just remember you'll soon be heaping it with dirt and tools, or maybe using it as a backyard animal train ride. So plan accordingly.

Fig. 1

Fig. 2

HOMEMADE ICE CREAM

If you could take childhood and compress it into a distinct taste, this, for me, would be it.

Homemade ice cream, tinged with sweetness and cream and just a hint of salt, always tastes like summer in the park, playing with friends, a good game of hide-and-seek, or climbing into a secret tree fort.

In other words, like childhood.

When I was younger, about eight or so, someone brought an ice-cream machine with a metal bucket and a crank to a picnic. The kids all took turns cranking the cream-filled metal tub around a bath of ice and salt, and then we got to eat straight from the tub. Every time my daughter and I make homemade ice cream, I'm reminded of that day and the deliciousness of summer.

I'm also reminded that you don't need a lot of stuff—tools, machines, adult supervision—to make something really fun.

Probably the greatest thing about this craft is that you very likely have everything you need in the fridge and the pantry already. It doesn't take a special skill or machine or recipe. It just takes a few household ingredients and a little time—maybe fifteen minutes tops.

Homemade ice cream has become a go-to play-date favorite or weekend afternoon treat for us. It has all sorts of possibilities and variations—from the simple to the extravagant—but the process is always easy and quick and sure to please.

HERE'S WHAT YOU NEED

- ☐ ½ cup whole milk (Half and half is best if you have it.)
- ☐ 1 tablespoon sugar
- ☐ 1 capful vanilla flavoring (or your favorite)
- ☐ Food coloring
- ☐ 2 Ziploc bags—one sandwich size and one freezer bag in gallon or two-gallon size
- ☐ Ice—lots!
- ☐ Salt—lots!
- ☐ 1 dish towel

HERE'S WHAT YOU DO

1 Mix the milk, sugar, flavoring, and food coloring in the small Ziploc bag and seal with as little air as possible in bag. Seriously, you are almost done. It's that simple. You've already done the hard part. Hope you're not too exhausted.

2 Fill the big Ziploc bag with ice and salt. The more the merrier.

3 Put the small bag in the large bag, seal, and then start shaking like you mean it. This is where the dish towel comes into play, as your hands will get pretty cold. Try leaving a bit of air in the big bag before you seal it, so that the ice and salt can move around and coat the smaller bag inside. If you want to let the ice rest on the small bag for a few minutes, go for it. But don't give up shaking altogether.

4 After about ten minutes, take out the small bag and . . . enjoy. You're done. That's it. Kitchen magician, that's what you are. Or at least what the kids will think anyway: "My dad, the Harry Potter of the kitchen." Every dude's dream.

5 Some people like to rinse off the small bag first, and sure, if you hate childhood, feel free to do it that way. Others like to eat it straight from the small bag, as you get little bits of salt with every taste. The sweet-salty thing will send you into fits of nostalgic bliss. *(See Fig. 1)*

DAD TIP

That's the basic recipe, but you can tinker with the milk or cream before you put it in the bag. For instance, instead of adding a capful of flavor, try simmering ginger or cinnamon sticks with the milk over the stove for about ten minutes. Then strain, cool, and use that milk to make the ice cream. What about orange cardamom? Simmer milk with orange peel and the spice for ten minutes . . . mmm. You can also alter the sugar amount to make it less cloying, although more sugar means a smoother texture. Have fun with it and experiment with a lot of batches. You can't really go wrong.

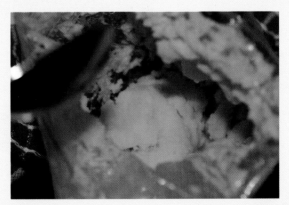

Fig. 1

HOMEMADE GOO SLIME

Remember those quarter gumball machines at the grocery store, the ones with little plastic containers filled with parachute men or mood rings or—my favorite—slime?

My poor mom. I hounded her to death during every grocery store outing.

"Can I have a quarter, mom? Please, please, *please*?"

Later, as a parent myself, I learned never to negotiate with terrorists, or as we call them now, children.

But back then, I was all about the slime. I'm sure it was made of horrible toxins or even people, like Soylent Green. But I just loved when I put a quarter into the machine and out popped a little ball of slime. You could stretch it, throw it, break it apart, or pretend you had a horrible cold and a sickly runny nose.

That goo was the stuff of memories.

So I was pretty excited when my daughter's school made homemade goo slime one day and she brought home the recipe. As an adult, I realized there's not much you can actually *do* with slime. With Play-Doh, at least you can make stuff. But slime just sort of oozes back into a blob.

Still, to kids, it's as magical as I remember—a slippery, slimy wonderland of disgusting possibility.

All told, it takes about five minutes to make, once you assemble your ingredients and have everything ready to go. Plus, you can have a little talk about science and goo polymers, those long-chain wonders of the molecule world. Or you can just pretend you have a giant booger.

Either way, fun times.

HERE'S WHAT YOU NEED

- ❏ Borax soap powder (20 Mule Team Borax)
- ❏ 1 cup water
- ❏ White glue
- ❏ Food coloring
- ❏ Some big bowls or containers

HERE'S WHAT YOU DO

1 Mix a heaping tablespoon of Borax soap powder with ½ cup of water.

2 In a separate, preferably bigger bowl or container, mix ½ cup white glue with the other ½ cup of water (Elmer's makes perfect-sized 4-ounce glue bottles so you can just empty the whole thing into your mixing bowl). Add your favorite food coloring to this container and stir it around until it's really smooth.

3 Now, here's the fun part. Pour your Borax mix into the colored mix. *(See Fig. 1)* Spoon that stuff around like a tornado. It should quickly begin to resemble scrambled eggs. The harder and faster you stir, the more amazing this next part will be. It looks like nothing's really happening or not much anyway—maybe a few lumps here and there or a hint of congealing. And then all of a sudden—*Boom!* The mix just breaks away from the sides of your stirring container and becomes this perfect, firm lump of goo. It is seriously magic (well, science—polymers, anyway) and has that "wow" factor kids always love.

DAD TIP

I've made thicker, better goo slime by increasing the amount of Borax and decreasing the amount of water slightly. If this first one doesn't work out for you or doesn't quite feel right, try adding more Borax and using less water. Just please, take the time to really stir it up well, otherwise the Borax remains grainy and the slime will, too.

4 When you're done, just plop it out and go to town. Stretch it, break it apart, watch it ooze back together into a floppy, oozy disc of awesomeness. When finished, store it in an airtight container. It lasts for a surprisingly long time and makes for a great, quick, and easy toy.

Fig. 1

SUPERHERO CAPES

Forget bank robbers and evil villains bent on world domination. If there really *were* superheroes, they would go after commercial cape makers for outrageous price gouging.

Seriously, most of the kid capes you find in stores are ridiculously overpriced pieces of fabric and glitter.

This is the beauty of crafting: You can make your own personalized cape with just two pieces of fabric, a little embellishment, and a sewing machine. But even if you *don't* have a sewing machine, you can still MacGyver up an old T-shirt into an excellent cape in about ten minutes. And sure, feel free to use duct tape if you'd like.

Look, I know the feeling. Store-bought capes look fun. Before my wife got me into sewing, I'd go into boutique kid stores and marvel at the amazing capes. They looked fantastic: sparkly, glittery, something a real superhero might wear.

After I learned to sew, however, I realized how preposterously easy it was to make those things and couldn't believe I almost shelled out $60 for something that costs less than $5 in materials. The super-great thing about doing it yourself is that you can personalize it any way you want: initials, logos, badges, you name it.

So grab some fabric and get accustomed to the sewing machine. Trust me, the kids will think *you're* the superhero after you whip up one of these.

HERE'S WHAT YOU NEED

(CAPE WITH FABRIC)

- ❏ Fabric—a yard (fabric is sold in yards) of your favorite color, preferably solid; or let the kid choose the color
- ❏ Embellishments—iron-on logos, initials, whatever you'd like
- ❏ Iron-on paper (So that if you don't have an iron-on logo already, you can make your own!)
- ❏ Bias tape (You can find this at your favorite craft or fabric store. Again, let the kid choose the color.)

TOOLS
- ❏ Sewing machine
- ❏ Iron
- ❏ Scissors
- ❏ Chalk

(CAPE WITH RECYCLED SHIRT)

- ❏ A T-shirt, maybe one with a cool logo
- ❏ Needle and thread
- ❏ Velcro bits if you have them (not absolutely necessary but nice if you don't like the idea of tying the cape around a neck)

TOOLS
- ❏ Scissors

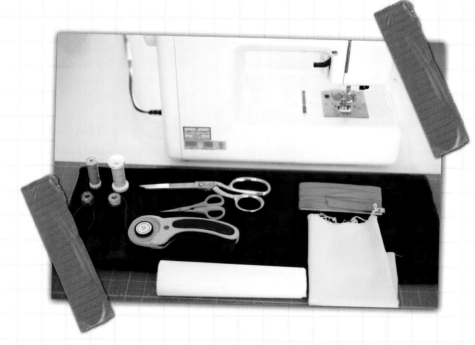

HERE'S WHAT YOU DO (*FABRIC*)

1 Take your yard of fabric and cut it in half and then place one half on top of the other. I prefer to use solid colors because it's easier, and any embellishments "pop" as opposed to getting mixed up with any fabric patterns.

2 Measure your child from neck to just below the hips—you probably don't want the cape to get too long, just so it doesn't trip her or get caught in things. But you can measure it to her toes if you'd like. It doesn't really matter. I just like the look of the hip-length kind. Anyway, there's your guide for size.

3 Using your personalized hip-to-neck length measurements as a guide, grab some chalk and trace out a cape design on the fabric, which should still be placed one piece on top of the other. When you trace, leave an extra inch at the bottom and the sides. For instance, if you measured from neck to hip and got 20", trace out 21" for length on the fabric. Make the sides an inch bigger than you want the finished product to be as well. When you sew later, this extra fabric magically *disappears*. As for the pattern, look, you know what a cape looks like: broad at the bottom, tapering up to the neck. It doesn't really have to be perfect, because sewing later on will provide the straight lines. Just trace a pattern onto the fabric.

4 Pin the pieces of fabric together, and cut it out in the pattern you've traced, making sure you're going through both pieces of fabric. When you're done cutting, you should have two identical, cape-shaped pieces of fabric. You are on the way!

5 If you'd like, now is the time to embellish one side of the cape. If you have an iron-on patch, go ahead and apply it. If you'd like to make a personalized cape with, say, the initials of your favorite, pint-sized crime fighter, take a swatch of different-colored fabric and follow the instructions on your iron-on paper. *(See Fig. 1)* You can buy this stuff cheap at any fabric store. All you do is iron a good amount on your swatch of fabric and then, once dry (thirty seconds), cut out the initials you'd like from the swatch. Then peel off the sticky paper and place the initials, sticky side down, on the cape where you want them. Iron them on. *Boom!* That's it. You can also sew them on for good measure and to prevent later fraying, but simple ironing should work fine.

6 Once your cape is personalized, here's the trick: Place the side you just embellished on the other cape-shaped fabric so that the embellishments are facing down. In other words, the embellished, personalized side should look as if it's inside out. Yes, exactly. It seems weird, but here comes the magic.

7 Pin the cape so that the bottom matches the bottom, the sides match the sides, and the neck matches the neck.

8 Now, you can begin sewing. Start at the neck and go down one side, and then sew the bottom before going up the side and stopping at the other side of the neck. The neck should remain un-sewn and open, as if you just made a really big pouch.

9 Take your scissors and cut off excess fabric around the edges. Don't get too close to your thread line but also don't leave too much fabric—¼" tops. *(See Fig. 2)*

10 Once it looks good to go, turn the fabric inside out. Now, your embellishments should be on the outside for all to see. Iron the corners and side to set the shape in place. This is the secret to sewing: 90 percent of it is ironing. Ironing makes everything look perfect.

11 Cut a long strip of bias tape—let's say 2'. Place the middle of the strip at the middle of the cape neck so that the ends of the

Fig. 1

Fig. 2

Fig. 3

bias tape form long ties. Almost done now. See how the tape opens up and forms a pocket sort of? Make sure you place the cape neck inside that pocket and then pin closed.

12. Now sew the bias tape closed all along the strip. *(See Fig. 3)* This process closes the cape neck and also provides the cape ties. If you'd like, you can make your own bias tape, but store bought is so much easier for those not familiar with sewing.

That's it. You just made your very own superhero cape. Well done!

If you don't have a sewing machine, here's a great way to take an old T-shirt and make your own cape.

HERE'S WHAT YOU DO (*RECYCLED SHIRT*)

1. Take your old T-shirt and flatten it out so that the logo is facing up. Once it's all smoothed out, cut around the neck of the shirt on the back, starting in the middle and ending where the shoulder hem meets the front of the neck. *(See Fig. 1)* In other words, only cut out the back side, not the front. The front will form your cape.

2. Once you have the neck cut out, cut down the front of your shirt to form a cape shape, making sure you keep the logo you want. *(See Fig. 2)* You don't even really need to trace any pattern if you don't want; just cut down the shirt from the neck to the bottom, angling out along the way. When you're done, you should have a cape

Fig. 1

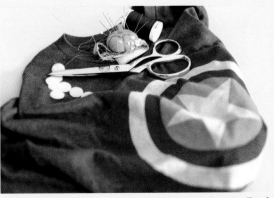

Fig. 2

that is wider at the bottom and then tapers to the neck. You can stop here and just use the neck pieces you cut out as the ties. Seriously, that's it. You're done. You now have an official T-shirt cape and this part probably took you all of two minutes. You can hem the sides and bottom if you'd like, or add some bias tape for design, but T-shirt fabric doesn't really fray much.

3 If you're uncomfortable using the neck as a tie, take some Velcro pieces and hand sew them in place to fit. This should take another five minutes. Should the cape get snagged on something during play, the Velcro breaks away easily.

So there you go: two kinds of capes. You never know when you'll have a super-hero emergency.

POPSICLE STICK BRIDGES

M any years ago I worked as a newspaper reporter, covering the construction of the new Bay Bridge in the San Francisco Bay Area. It hit all my favorite nerd parts: construction, engineering, design.

I was in dork heaven.

While there were some things I didn't miss about the job after I moved on, I was definitely sad to leave behind the nitty-gritty details of a big-truck engineering marvel. It seemed I learned something new every day. But the thing that really stuck for years and years was the different designs of bridges and what engineering forces make them work.

I found it all just fascinating.

When my daughter got old enough to start asking questions about the bridge construction she saw near home or when we were traveling, I was proud to have some answers. It seems practically everywhere we go, we see bridges. If this happens to you, I have the perfect craft project to show the key differences between the major kinds.

On a rainy afternoon, my daughter and I raided her art bin for Popsicle sticks and glue and tape and twine, and then we set about creating a suspension bridge, a self-anchored suspension span (the new Bay Bridge design), and a cable-stay bridge. When we finished the project, I posted photos online at the *San Francisco Chronicle* parenting blog I write for. Caltrans, the state agency overseeing construction, saw our designs and liked them so much they invited us out to the bridge to see the work up close.

Again, dork heaven. ▶

I'll lay out the differences between the bridges here, but if you're not interested, you can go right to the how-to on making a suspension span bridge out of everyday kitchen and art supplies. It's a great way to not only get your hands all glue-y and tape-y but also pass on some engineering lessons.

Here are the differences between the bridges we built:

- **Suspension span.** Think Golden Gate Bridge. There are two main cables that are anchored into the ground on each side. The cables are laced across the two main towers. From those two main cables, smaller cables connect to the road deck, holding it up. This type of bridge is built with the towers first, then the cables, and then the road deck.

- **Self-anchored suspension span.** This is the new Bay Bridge. Like a regular suspension span, it uses a main cable from which smaller cables are draped down to the road. Instead of two main cables that are anchored into the ground on either side of the bridge, there is only one main cable, and it goes under the bridge and then over the tower and under the bridge again, making an enormous loop. Smaller cables are attached to this main cable and connected to the road.

- **A cable-stay bridge.** These always look like giant fans. Instead of using main cables to hold up the little cables, the little cables are attached directly to the towers from the road.

See? Nerd heaven. Now, on to the craft.

If Popsicle sticks alone don't do the trick for this sort of project, add twine, or tape, or Lego blocks. If your passion is building architecture, go to town on creating a skyscraper instead. But if your dork bells go off at the sight of bridges, this one is for you. For this project, we're going to build a suspension span.

HERE'S WHAT YOU NEED

- ❏ Popsicle sticks
- ❏ Tape—duct, Scotch, whatever you have
- ❏ Twine

TOOLS

- ❏ Scissors

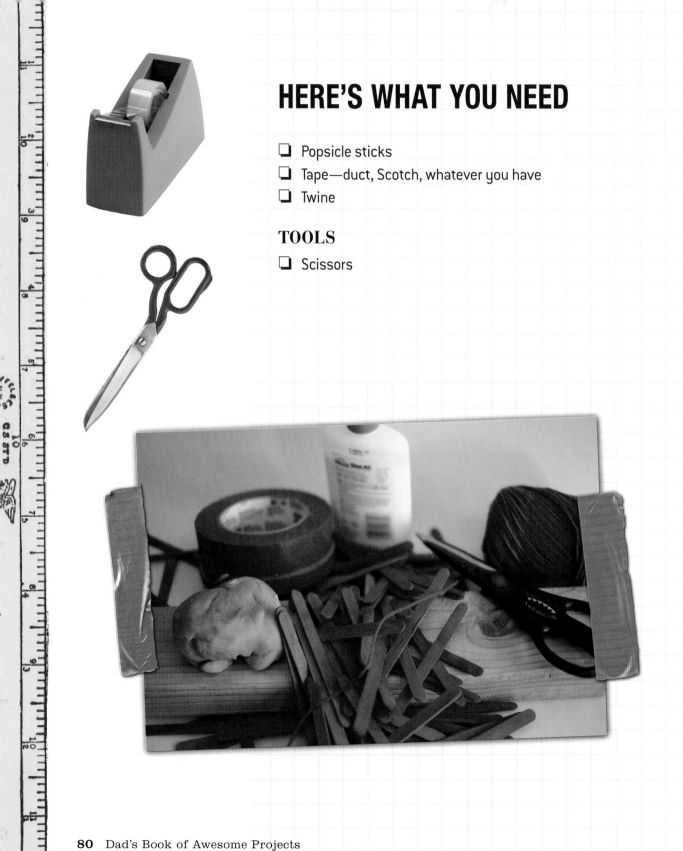

HERE'S WHAT YOU DO

1 Build two towers out of sticks. *(See Fig. 1)* Let the kid choose the kind and type and size. If it falls, try again. This is science in action! If you want, replicate the Golden Gate Bridge by using a couple of photos as models. At first, you might want to find bridge pictures online and try to make a smaller model, using tape to hold everything together.

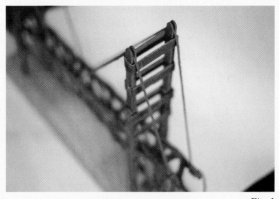

Fig. 1

2 Now build a road deck—something big enough to connect to with twine but small enough so the main towers can hold it up. *(See Fig. 2)* You may have to tinker with a few different designs, but I like to use the triangle design you see so often on road decks. There's a reason you see so many triangles on real bridges—they work!

Fig. 2

3 Drape the twine over the towers and secure the twine with tape on, say, the floor or your work surface. Pull it as tight as possible, as these main cables will carry a lot of the weight load. You may have to go back and fix your towers. And that's cool. Physics, yo! It's not just for falling asleep in high school anymore.

Fig. 3

4 Now, get your road deck in place with tape and then tape or tie smaller pieces of twine from the main cable to the road deck. *(See Fig. 3)* That's it. You're done. You may need a lot of string. Or you may need a lot of tape. Or you may need a lot of both. Just keep tinkering with it until it feels sturdy enough to support itself.

DAD TIP

If your child is anything like mine, the bridge will look a little . . . well, special. That's fine. The older kids get, the cooler and more realistic the bridge will look. I just like to let the kids get a quick lesson in engineering before trying to replicate the different bridges. If you want to work on your own bridge at the same time, go for it!

CARDBOARD CREATIONS

Every winter when I was a kid, I would eyeball our neighborhood park as soon as the rains came.

"Someday," I would think to myself, "someday I will sail these seas."

When I finally set sail as a child, it was everything I dreamed it would be.

Of course, the "seas" in this case was the sandbox—a bastion of loamy grit hemmed in by a circle of concrete and flooded with the brown, sludgy remains of recent storms and who knows what else.

As an adult, I noticed our neighborhood park was struck by the same flooding each year. I told my wife about my long-harbored plans to build a sailing vessel for the seasonal playground seas, and she immediately put her hands on her hips.

"Sounds fun," she said. "But with whose child? Because it's not going to be mine!"

Of course, our daughter was an infant then, so it didn't seem possible that she would one day become the salty, toddler-sized Captain Ahab of San Francisco's flooded parks.

Time passed, our daughter grew older, and still the floods came—until, one day, using a spare cardboard box, a lot of duct tape, and a used floor mop for an oar, we finally built our boat and took to the miniature ocean.

It was everything I envisioned. The child beamed with delight, steering her craft atop the one-foot-deep waters just as I had done so many years ago at my own flooded playground.

Cardboard, duct tape, imagination, and a little elbow grease. What more do you really need in life?

Of course, you don't need to build a boat. That was just *my* fantasy.

You can craft anything you want and let your child use his imagination. Just please, think outside the box. A little cutting, a generous amount of duct tape, some crayons or markers and butcher's twine, and suddenly you can have the greatest castle ever built, or a rocket ship, or just maybe a near-perfect replica of the *Pequod*, Ahab's famous whaling ship.

HERE'S WHAT YOU NEED

- ❏ Cardboard (pretty much any big box will do)
- ❏ Duct tape
- ❏ 2 or 3 large garbage bags
- ❏ 2 or 3 paper towel cardboard rollers
- ❏ Old mop—Swiffer or something else you're done with around the house
- ❏ Twine, rope, dental floss (anything you might need for sails or rope nets)
- ❏ Crayons, markers, anything to decorate

TOOLS

- ❏ Scissors or a box cutter

HERE'S WHAT YOU DO

Use your imagination.

You heard me. Get going. Cut, fold, tape, shape, decorate. Break out your hands and go to town.

Okay, okay, fine. So you want something more in the way of directions. I hear you.

Here's how I built a really cool floating boat that managed to stay afloat for more than ten minutes.

1 Find a large rectangular box and open up one of the ends. Let the cardboard know who's the boss. That's the biggest part. Don't be afraid to fold it and tape it and tie it until your heart's content.

2 Fold the end flaps up to resemble a ship's bow. Duct-tape the ever-living jebus out of that thing. *(See Fig. 1)*

3 Duct-tape all the seams around the sides and any part you think may hit the water. You can tape up the bottom if you want. Even better, duct-tape the garbage bag to the bottom for extra water protection. *(See Fig. 2)* But look, it's cardboard. It's going to sink eventually, so I like to just let the water in when the water wants to come in. Half the fun is abandoning ship anyway.

4 So once you have a ship shape, tape together the paper towel rollers to add a mast. I used garbage bags for a "sail." I took an old Swiffer mop and covered it with duct tape and used that for an oar.

5 Take the monstrosity to your nearest flooded park and enjoy. It works best if the kid is kneeling, as opposed to standing up. And please, don't go in deep water if your little sailor can't swim.

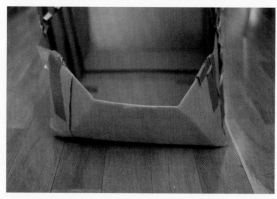

Fig. 1

Fig. 2

TINKER BOARD

It's difficult to reach back into the mental ether and draw out complete scenes from early childhood, but I do have fond and vivid memories of playing with . . . something.

Okay, so maybe not fond. *Or* vivid. Vague is more like it.

I have *vague* memories of playing with something. But whatever it was, it was really, really cool.

It was some sort of plastic board or table doohickey with lots of flaps and dials and wheels to turn. I think it made noise, which probably delighted me to no end but made my parents want to jump off the nearest bridge.

The point is, it was awesome.

I searched for something similar for my daughter to play with, but as I only had vague memories of this device, it was hard to find. Then one day my wife told me about the "tinker box" her grandpa made. It was a simple, hollow wooden box to which he had attached a bunch of household gadgets—hinges and door latches, locks and slide bolts. It sounded like the Ron Swanson (remember him, from *Parks and Recreation*?) of toddler toys, and I immediately started to think of my own design.

The only problem was we lived in a big-city apartment. I didn't have a lot of tools, certainly not a workshop. It was difficult to find the time and space to come up with a tinker box.

"Why not use a cutting board?" my wife asked.

Genius.

HERE'S WHAT YOU NEED

❑ A cutting board (Yes, any plank will do, but I like the re-use factor of an old cutting board.)

❑ Hardware—chain locks, hinges, hasps, slide bolts . . . whatever you want to install or have around

❑ Screws—½", or long enough to keep the hardware in place while short enough not to poke through the other end of the board

❑ Stain or paint (optional; if you think a kid might lick all over this thing, don't even bother)

TOOLS

❑ Drill (You can use a screwdriver but drills are faster and cooler—yay power!)

❑ Sandpaper, just to smooth things up a bit

HERE'S WHAT YOU DO

1 If you'd like, give the cutting board a good sanding and a simple stain to pretty it up. Or just go with it as it is. Lots of cutting boards are already polished and pretty. Plus, some have "gripper" bottoms, which prevent the board from sliding around on the counter. These are awesome for tinker boards.

2 Take all your hardware goods and arrange them on the cutting board. *(See Fig. 1)* Better yet, let the kid arrange them. Make sure you have room to slide the bolts or open hasps or close hinges. Give yourself a couple of inches between each item. You don't have to fill the entire board—just enough to make it interesting. Chain door bolts are always a hit, by the way.

3 Once you're satisfied with the layout, screw everything in. I found that ½"-long screws seem to do the job and also don't poke through. *(See Fig. 2)* Most cutting boards are made up of several pieces of wood pressed and glued together. Those seams provide great guides for keeping everything in line. Just try not to screw into the seams themselves; otherwise, the board could crack. This is a great step to teach the proper use of a drill and to let an older kid feel like she is making something cool for a younger sibling.

4 When finished, hand over the tinker board to your favorite toddler and enjoy your awesome work and the happy hours that come with flipping hinges and unlocking

Fig. 1

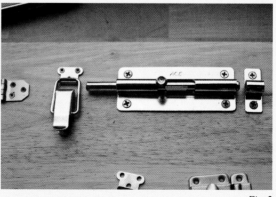

Fig. 2

hasps. No, I mean it. You're done. That's it. I could have made this more complicated and told you to go craft a beautiful box— and indeed, that would make for an awesome project if you're down for it or if the tinker board goes over especially well. But what could be more simple and elegant and fun than a toy you crafted from a used kitchen aid and some castoff hardware? The first time I finished a tinker board, I thought it was too simple, too easy. But toddlers don't know that. They just have fun with it for *hours*.

DAD TIP

My wife was concerned about "pinching" with all the hinges and slides and hasps, etc. And yes, that can happen. My take on that is sure, your kid or the kid you give this to could get pinched, but probably only once or twice until they learn *not* to pinch themselves. Still, you might consider this a present for toddlers, as opposed to babies who just want to shove everything in their mouths anyway.

WOODEN SWORD

I was maybe five or six. We were at Disneyland. In Frontierland, we stopped in at some general store—it was probably *called* the General Store—but, again, I was young. It's all sort of hazy.

What really stands out is just the mind-boggling array of weaponry and treasure: BB guns, cap guns, rifles, raccoon-skin caps, rubber knives, eye patches, and buckets of gold coins and bins of colored jewels.

It was a veritable arsenal of childhood joy.

In reality, everything was probably as it is today: cheap goods made of plastic and shipped from some overseas, lead-perfumed factory. But in my memories, it remains a trove of adventure, a supply store for all possible childhood fantasies.

I really wanted to offer that sense of adventure and fantasy to my child, and nothing can quite provide that like a sword—an honest-to-goodness, old-school, homemade, wooden sword.

A wooden sword is a vehicle for stories and play; put one in your hand and all of a sudden, you're a knight, or a pirate, or a soldier out-fighting make-believe armies.

Yes, to be sure, you can also put your eye out or do some damage. Many schools frown on weapons of any kind for fear of violent play—but take those kids on a hike and I flat guarantee you that within five minutes they'll pick up a stick and use it as a sword.

Swords must hark back to some instinctual survival trait, so why not let kids get it out under your supervision? All of this is to say, you might want to hold off on this one until you feel the time is right. You know your kids better than anyone. But when it is the right time, this is a fantastic way to spend an afternoon and to prepare for all your adventures to come.

HERE'S WHAT YOU NEED

- ❏ Some wood (Unused bed slats work perfectly!)
- ❏ Wood stain
- ❏ Optional: Old leather shoelaces

TOOLS

- ❏ A saw (Yes, it's possible to use a handsaw, but if you have a jigsaw or a band saw, you can do the hard part in minutes.)
- ❏ Sandpaper

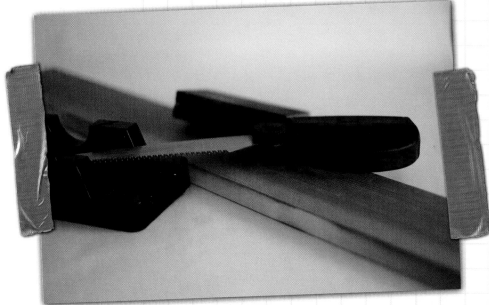

HERE'S WHAT YOU DO

1 Find some wood. Make it nice—or at least something solid and long enough to provide both a handle and a blade, about two feet or so. Our favorite pirate sword was built using an unused bed slat from the bunk bed I refurbished for my daughter's bedroom. But you can also find a nice piece of cherry or oak or walnut from your local hardware store, if you don't have something lying around. Here's the key, however: Don't use anything thicker than, say, an inch. The kids should be able to easily fit their hands around the handle.

2 Once you have a nice piece of wood ready to go, draw an outline of a handle, a hilt, and the blade. If you're using a jigsaw or a band saw, you can get a little fancier and draw a great pirate cutlass. If you're using a handsaw, stick with a straight blade that forms a blunt diamond tip at the top.

3 Now, start cutting. It's really as easy as following your drawing: Cut out the handle, leave the hilt in place, then cut the blade. *(See Fig. 1)* The great thing about this craft is that if the cuts don't look all that great, you don't need to worry about it:

You can always sand away any imperfections. My new-cut swords always look like half-complete, jagged messes. But that's where the next step comes into play.

4 The cutting should be relatively easy and quick, depending on the tools at your disposal. For the sanding, however, really take your time. Here is where you can sand away any cutting flaws. (Of course, if you also take the time with the cutting, you won't have so many flaws.) On the blade itself, make sure to go over the edges really well. You can sand them to a nice, round, comfortable edge that will keep everyone safe. Same goes for the tip.

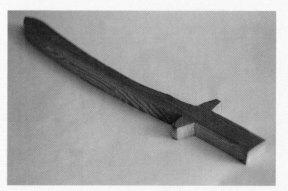

Fig. 1

5 Once you're happy with the sanding—the blade, the hilt, the handle—and your sword has really taken shape, take it one step further and apply a nice wood stain. This adds the perfect old-fashioned sheen—and also helps to destroy any remaining flaws. Stain, wipe, stain again if needed, and then sand very lightly. If you'd like, add a coat of furniture polish after the stain is set and dry to really bring out the shine, but that's up to you.

6 If you'd like, wrap and tie old leather shoelaces around the handle to give a better grip and design. But that's optional.

7 After the staining, you're good to go. Have a talk about safety and then go off and find your own adventures. All you really need is a great imagination.

DAD TIP

If possible, let the kids draw the sword design on the wood and do most of the sanding. If they're old enough, you can coach them through the cutting as well. I've found that the more the kids help out, the more they actually play with the swords and the prouder they feel to wield them.

HIDDEN BOOK STASH

When I was a kid, I pulled up the carpet in my bedroom. It took a long time and annoyed my parents *completely* when they discovered the ripped-up flooring.

But that wasn't the worst part of the endeavor. The worst part was removing a corner of the carpet and discovering underneath a flat sheet of stupid plywood.

I was so disappointed.

I'm still not sure exactly what I was expecting—a giant hole, a pathway to China, the place where Morlocks went during the day. (I wasn't the brightest child.) But what I was after was a secret hiding spot to call my own.

Growing up with two older brothers, you learn to hoard things: candy, money, anything shiny or of potential use, but mostly candy. After the carpet fiasco, I started hiding things in the heating vents. When winter came, I was overjoyed that my room suddenly filled with the aroma of chocolate and sugar. That is, until I realized where the delightful smell was coming from, lifted the vent, and discovered a puddle of melted candy. (Again, not bright.)

Had I learned to make this secret hidden book stash, I would have solved so many problems and stayed out of trouble. It's the perfect hiding spot for little treasures—a special trove for your child to call her own. Because it's made from a real book, it blends in perfectly on a bookshelf. And you can customize the inside any way you want.

So do the kid in your life a favor and make this now—or at least before winter comes.

HERE'S WHAT YOU NEED

- ❑ An old book—anything you'll never actually need, as long as it's thick (at least 3")
- ❑ Rubber band
- ❑ Glue
- ❑ A piece of cardboard or decorative paper
- ❑ Crayons for decorating (optional)

TOOLS

- ❑ X-Acto knife or craft knife (a box cutter also works)
- ❑ Paintbrush for glue

HERE'S WHAT YOU DO

1 Find a book. That's the first part. It has to be pretty thick, or at least thick enough to hide things in. Hardcovers work best. As a writer and lover of reading, I feel conflicted about this project, as I dislike ripping up books. But the payoff is worth it, big time. Plus, this project can allow you to act as a critic and rip up that crappy book you hated (oh, god, if you take a box cutter to this one . . .).

2 Flip open the book about a quarter of the way and use the rubber band to hold those pages to the front book cover. You'll need them all later to keep the book disguise intact.

3 Now you have the book open to about page 100 or so. Paint some glue on the outsides of the pages on the right side of the book—the thick part. Just brush some on the sides of the pages, not the part with words. Let dry. If you use a light enough coat, it dries pretty quickly.

4 Take one of your crayons and outline a rectangle on the open page on the right side of the book. Again, the thicker part. This will be the part you cut out. Leave about two inches from the binding, and about an inch on all the other sides. You

don't have to be exact. Just make a rectangle pattern to cut.

5 Now, you can begin cutting. Of all the projects in the book, this is the most dangerous thing, I believe. So please, be super careful. You may want to see a lot of progress right away, so you try to dig in deep with the knife or box cutter. Don't do that. Too much pressure, and the book slips and the cutter gouges out your wrist. Not fun. So take your time with this. Start with one side of your rectangle and cut a few pages at a time. Then go deeper. Then go deeper. Again, take your time. Within about five minutes you should be ready to move on to the next side of the rectangle.

6 Once all the cutting is done, remove the rectangle of paper. You should have a perfect little hiding spot in the book. Yes, all the edges will look weird and jagged, and the binding area can be a pain to cut. But don't worry; you're about to make it all look perfect.

7 When all stray pieces are cut away, brush some glue on the outside edges again and on the inside edges you just cut. Let it dry before moving on to the next step.

8 Once dry, take one of the pages that you secured to the left side of the book. Now let it fall across the right side of the book, where the hole is now. Smooth it out. It should hide the hole. You may have to fold up the left side of the book a touch to make the page fit perfectly. Go for it.

9 Once that page is in place, cut out a rectangle that is much, much smaller than the one you created for the hole. Once you have a small rectangle in that one page, cut a diagonal line from each corner stretching to the corners of your hidden stash rectangle. *(See Fig. 1)*

10 See how you just created four little flaps out of that small rectangle? Take those flaps and fold them down over your big rectangle. (See photo.) Glue the flaps to the bottom of your hidden stash hole. This process should hide any jagged edges or cut marks from the hole. If it doesn't work the first time, simply cut out that flap-making page and use another one from the left side. You'll get it.

11 At this point, unsecure the pages on the left side and you can call it a day. The little flaps should provide the finished look you need for the hole. But if you really want to make this a special, personalized hidden stash—and why wouldn't you?—cut a piece of cardboard or decorative paper to fit the bottom of the stash hole and glue it in place. Then you can color it or write anything you want. "Keep out!" seems to send the perfect message.

Fig. 1

ROPE SWING

If you've ever lived near a lake or near some woods or played in a creek as a child, you probably know all this already. Some of the most fun I remember from childhood comes from nothing more than some rope and a tree. There's no limit to the amount of excitement kids can have with these. In fact, my wife's cousin, a Boy Scout troop leader, is fond of saying the best way to get kids outdoors is to toss out some rope and some wood and then lock the door behind them.

"You probably won't see them for hours!"

If you're looking to get your child into the amazing world of rope and wood—the gateway craft material for hours of blissful, imaginative play—this is the perfect project to start with. You and the kid, or kids, are sure to have a great time.

HERE'S WHAT YOU NEED

- ❏ Rope—length depends on tree limb you choose
- ❏ Twine
- ❏ Rock
- ❏ Duct tape
- ❏ Tree limb
- ❏ Scrap piece of wood 1' × 6' (for optional seat)

TOOLS (ONLY FOR OPTIONAL SEAT)

- ❏ Big drill bit
- ❏ Sandpaper
- ❏ Saw if you need to cut scrap wood

HERE'S WHAT YOU DO

1 If the tree limb you want to use as a swing beam is low enough, you don't even need the twine and tape and rock. Just chuck the rope over the limb, being sure it's out away from the trunk, and then proceed to rope-tying steps.

2 If the tree limb is really high, you'll need some twine and tape and a rock. (Also, you'll need some longer rope. Choose your limb based on rope availability.) Unreel a lot of twine—enough to get over the tree limb and back to the ground—then tie the twine to one end of your rope. Tape the other end of the twine to the rock. *(See Fig. 1)*

3 Now, you or your little helper can toss the twine-taped rock over the limb. Then use the twine to pull the swing rope up over the limb and back down. Difficult, right? Please. But here's the deal. You have to be sure the rope is as far out on the limb as safely possible. Test it with your own weight first to be sure the limb can hold before you start tying. Again, make sure the point where you will lock the rope in place on the limb is as far away as you can safely be from the trunk of the tree; otherwise your afternoon will sound like this: "Yay! Fun. Woohoo!" *Thunk!*

4 Once you're happy with the placement of your rope over the tree limb, it's time to secure it in place. Now, I've seen all sorts of crazy knots and recommendations, but I've found that a simple hitch works perfectly. *(See Fig. 2)* Plus, most of the other knots make it impossible for you to get your rope back once it's tied in place.

Fig. 1

Fig. 2

Using a hitch allows you to secure the rope swing and also get your rope back when you want it. Make a loop with one end of your rope and then cross the loop end over your rope, tuck under, and pull the loop back out. *Boom!* You should now have one end of the rope that has a loop hitch and the other end free of knots.

5 Remember that twine you used to throw the rope over the tree? Untape it and tie one end to that loop you just created. This will come in handy later.

6 Now, run the non-knotted end of rope through the loop and pull the non-knotted end until the loop begins the climb toward the tree limb. Don't worry about the twine getting in the way. You'll do something with it soon. Just try your best to not shift the rope toward the tree trunk. You may have to shake or pull or twist the rope to get the knot to the top of the tree limb.

7 Now your loop hitch should be at your tree limb, or close to it, and the rope should be dangling to the ground with your twine. Awesome. Let's get the twine out of the way. Tie it around the tree trunk, going as high as you can. (If you'd like and have the strength for it, you can climb the rope a bit and tie the twine on the rope high enough to stay out of the way.)

8 See how the twine's still attached to the loop up there near the tree? If you want to retrieve your rope when you're done swinging, just pull on the twine until the loop wiggles free and starts to come down. Be gentle at first and then, once you can, pull the loop to the ground, untie your knots, and go home with your rope. Easy peasy lemon cheesy. **Note**: If you're just going to leave the rope swing in place forever, don't even bother with the twine.

9 You can stop there if you'd like. Or you can tie some knots in the dangling rope for foot loops or hand holds. A rope by itself is a good enough swing. But if you want to add a seat or a foot stand, it's time to break out your scrap wood.

10 Cut the wood to a good size—no more than a foot. Then sand the board like crazy, especially if you're going to be sitting on it.

11 Use your drill to make a hole in the middle wide enough to accommodate the rope end. Pass the dangling rope through the hole, tying it off at the bottom as high as you'd like the swing to be. And that's it.

You now have a great rope swing you and the kids can take with you on hikes or to the lake.

BOW AND ARROWS

I don't know about you, but when I was younger I was obsessed with Robin Hood. Not so much the whole thing about living in a forest with a bunch of dudes in tights, but you know, that's cool, too.

No, I was obsessed with his mad bow-and-arrow skills.

I can't even tell you how many dopey daydreams I had about winning the hands of so many neighborhood girls by guiding an arrow through *another* arrow, just like Robin Hood.

What? I was a total nerd, okay?

Whatever *your* reasons are for wanting to make a bow and arrow, I think we can all agree on this: It's whittlin' time.

That's the great thing about making your own bow-and-arrow set. All you need is a good stick and a good knife, maybe a few kitchen supplies and voilà! All of a sudden you're in the backyard, trying to win imaginary target matches in your own Sherwood Forest.

What can be better than that?

HERE'S WHAT YOU NEED

❏ A long stick—at least 30"
❏ Kitchen twine
❏ Dowels—Arrow-sized; use what you can find.
❏ Found feathers
❏ Pencil eraser tips
❏ Optional: Old leather shoelaces

TOOLS

❏ Saw
❏ A good sharp knife or crafting razor
❏ Glue
❏ Duct tape

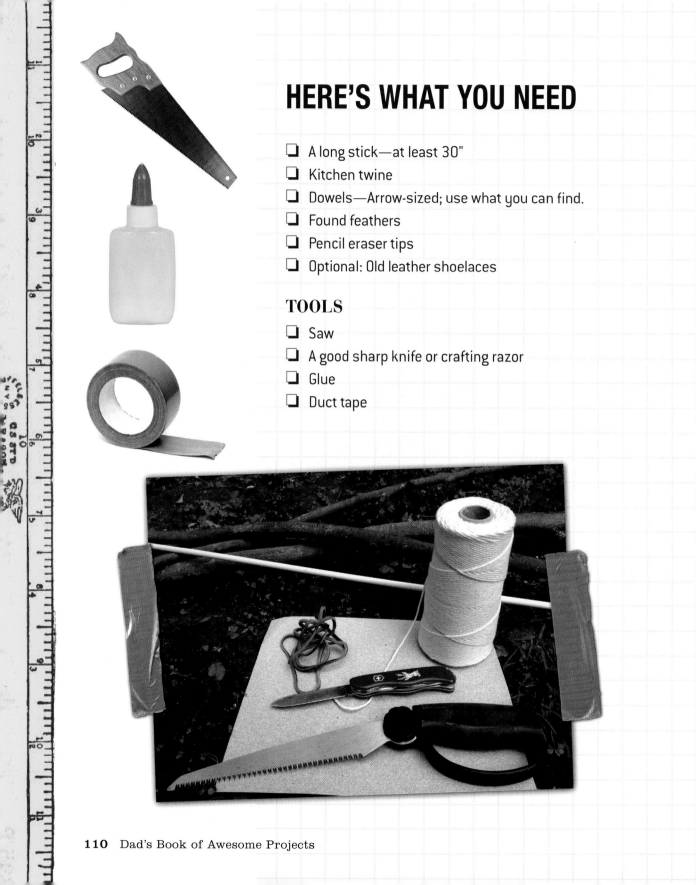

HERE'S WHAT YOU DO

1 To paraphrase the great Yogi Berra, 90 percent of this craft is all about finding the perfect stick for a bow, while the other half involves getting it ready for shooting. When we go on hikes, we like to keep our eyes open for the perfect stick. It's at least 30" long. It doesn't snap when bent—this is key! It looks thick enough for a kid to hold but not too thick for bending. You know what a bow looks like. When you bend your stick, you want it to be able to reach that bow shape and then snap back to a straight stick. Don't worry about finding a perfect "bow-shaped" stick, as a pre-bent stick won't supply the tension you need to actually shoot an arrow. Just find a good straight stick that will bend but not snap, that your child can easily hold, and that has ends thick enough to carve a few notches into.

2 Once you have your stick in hand, it's time to get it the right size. Don't snap it. Instead, break out a handsaw and cut it down to about 30" in length.

3 Now it's whittlin' time! I don't know why this always excites me so much. Maybe because it's such an old-school, nostalgic thing to do. How often do you get to whittle in your everyday life? I love it. The goal here is to get rid of any bark, twigs, leaves, or anything that will get in your way or that you don't want on the finished product. Hold your stick in one hand, and use your knife to scrape *away* from you. *(See Fig. 1)* Again, this is key for safety reasons. Move your knife away from you, as you scrape the stick. Let the kids try this and teach them the safe way to do it.

Fig. 1

Fig. 2

4 Now you have a pretty good-looking stick. It's time to get it ready for your bow string. Cut two notches on either side of each end, about an inch from the tip and angling in toward the middle of your bow. *(See Fig. 2)*

5 All that's left to do is tie your string. If you happen to have deer guts taking up space somewhere and the know-how to turn sinew into bow strings, by all means, do that. If not, simple kitchen twine will do the trick. Loop your twine around the two notches on one end of the bow and tie a good knot. Now, pull the string tight and loop it around the notches at the other end of your bow. Your stick should still be more or less straight. Be sure to pull the string super tight before tying your last knot.

6 Almost done. Now that you have your string knotted around the bow, have the kid take a practice pull or two. Find the place where it's most comfortable for a grip and then lace around that area your with old leather shoelaces and tie into place. This is optional, but it does give a nice old-timey look to the bow. *(See Fig. 3)*

7 Now it's time to make a few arrows. Take a dowel that's arrow-sized and grippable ($\frac{5}{16}$" or slightly smaller works great, but use what you have or can find), and cut it to about 14" to 16"in length. (Test how far back your kid can pull the bow string from the bow and then add a few inches to that for arrow size.)

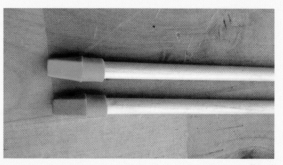

Fig. 4

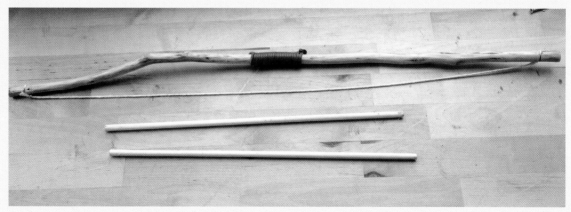

Fig. 3

8 Carve a notch in one end of the arrow. The bow string should fit into this notch.

 9 On the notch end, tape or glue some feathers (another great thing to find while hiking) to serve as the fletching, which keeps the arrow flying true.

10 On the other end, glue your pencil eraser on the dowel as a "tip." *(See Fig. 4)*

 **DAD TIP**

Look, if you're in some airplane crash in the wilderness and you need to whittle down some arrows from twigs and sticks to hunt for meat, you could do that. But if, like me, you have a youngish kid who's not quite ready to face any survivalist scenarios or might just accidentally take out someone's eyeball, you should probably stick with this method.

Wait until your arrows are dry and then have at it. Who knows? Maybe your child will get good enough to split another arrow through the middle. A kid can dream.

GARDEN HERB PLANTER

I'm not the best person to take advice from when it comes to anything green and plant-y. But if, like me, you like to slowly kill plants or herbs through casual neglect, this is the project for you!

I kid, I kid.

Herb garden planters are easy to make and to maintain—so easy that even *I* can do it.

And I've found that building a small herb garden not only makes a great present for the chef in your life but also saves a metric boatload of money on all the fancy herbs you no longer have to buy from the store. Plus, you can build this herb garden for just about *free*—my favorite number.

I got all the wood for our kitchen herb garden planters by hitting up the local hardware store for leftover wood pallets—those ancient, creaky wooden squares that stores use to stack and ship heavy products. Chances are your hardware or grocery store will just about write you a letter of appreciation and maybe offer some discounts if you ask to take a pallet off their hands. I've always been able to find a store dying to give them away so they don't have to pay someone to come take them.

Yes, you can go buy some wood for this. But why? A few minutes with a wood pallet and a hammer will give you all the wood you need and provide a great lesson on re-use. More than that, the wood often looks old and rustic, lending a country-like feel to any finished herb garden.

HERE'S WHAT YOU NEED

- ❏ A wood pallet
- ❏ Screws or nails (about 1½" long)
- ❏ Soil
- ❏ Rocks
- ❏ Herbs (with roots)
- ❏ Paint (optional)
- ❏ Thin metal wire and thick screw (optional)

TOOLS

- ❏ Hammer
- ❏ Saw
- ❏ Drill (if using screws)
- ❏ Measuring tape
- ❏ Wood glue
- ❏ Work gloves

HERE'S WHAT YOU DO

1 This is the cool part. You're going to need to take apart the slats on the wood pallet. Think of this as a controlled destruction derby and have some fun. You're going to want to take off the wood without damaging it beyond use. You'll need to hammer the back of a slat, near any nails, until it comes loose enough for you to pull the nails and free the slat. *(See Fig. 1)* Repeat until you have three good, long slats of the same size.

2 At this point, you're going to saw the wood into the lengths you want. Four 12" lengths for the sides and two 12" lengths for the bottom makes a manageable box. Cut the end pieces the same height as your finished sides. But wait. Can you just *not* cut the wood at all and create one long herb garden? Why yes! Yes you can! The only reason we chose this design was so that we could hang it on a rail outside our kitchen. By all means, feel free to use any lengths and widths you want.

3 If you're going to stack one piece of wood on top of the other to make a taller herb garden, you'll also need four tiny strips of wood you can use to join your sides together. They should be about 1" wide and the same height as the sides. *(See Fig. 2)*

4 Once you have all your wood, lay down the long lengths of your side pieces and match them up. Lay the inch-long connector pieces across the slats several inches from each end. Screw or nail those into place to create the two taller side pieces.

5 Now that you have your sides and your end pieces, you can assemble your box. Don't worry about the bottom just yet. Put the sides and end pieces together, with the end pieces inside the longer side pieces. *(See Fig. 3)* See how it works? Excellent. Add some wood glue now in the appropriate places to seal it all in place.

6 If you're in charge of hammering and drilling, you can probably get right to it. If your little helper will be in charge of hammering, wait a bit for the glue to dry so that the wood will be more secure.

7 Sink screws or nails at the end of each side piece, going into the end pieces. Four screws or nails on each side is plenty. *(See Fig. 4)* Be careful not to let any tips poke through anywhere, as you'll probably be sending the kiddos out to pick herbs in the future. They might get hurt, but more important, bloody herbs are not delicious.

Fig. 1

Fig. 2

Fig. 3

Fig. 4

Fig. 5

8 At this point, your box is in fine, sturdy shape. But you still need a bottom. Lay the slats across the bottom and screw or nail them into place. Don't worry about gaps. In fact, add small gaps if you can. These will allow water to drain all the way through and keep the soil nice and dainty for the herbs. (See? I am not really a plant murderer.)

9 Once your bottom is on, you're done. You can paint it if you'd like or do anything else you want to make it fit your space best. Then fill it with rocks at the bottom for drainage, add soil, and then pack in your herbs. I find a box of this size allows for two kinds of herbs just fine. Longer boxes obviously allow for more herbs.

10 If you're going to hang this bad boy somewhere, drill two small holes in the back and pass your thin metal wire through the holes. *(See Fig. 5)* Twist your wire ends together to form a loop. Drill in a thick screw where you want to hang the box, and then loop your wire around the screw once you've done all the planting.

DAD TIP

For what it's worth, I've found that mint and rosemary are particularly hardy and resistant to my attempts to casually destroy them.

WEEKEND 2 PROJECTS

BIRDHOUSE

When I was a boy, my family would head to Michigan every summer to visit my grandparents. This usually meant lots of ice cream and trips to the candy store and endless hours of Slip 'N Slide in the backyard, some of my favorite childhood memories.

It also meant serious bird watching.

My grandparents were obsessed with birds, setting up baths and houses and feeders before huddling inside with a good pair of binoculars at the rear window. I spent sixteen or so summers with them, spying on the natural world from the comfort of their dining room table. Now that my grandparents are gone, I can't look at a birdhouse or a birdbath without thinking of all the fun we had counting robins and jays and cardinals. It's probably a cliché to say this is one of life's "simple pleasures," but I'm grateful to have had that time with my grandparents and am grateful that their love of birds provided us all with so many rich memories.

Even here in the big city where I now live, the bird watching is quite amazing. Our backyard neighbor has an ancient oak tree that attracts everything from jays to crows to robins. One time, I saw an owl swoop low through the twilight. It was like watching a whisper in flight—just magical.

With a child of my own now, I wanted to share the simple, easy pleasure of bird watching.

So we built our own birdhouse.

This is a simple, clean-looking, mid-twentieth-century-motif model meant to offer a touch of art to any backyard, while also providing the perfect home for small birds—all while not requiring much more than a good saw, a drill, and some wood. On hikes, I've noticed that the birdhouses nature centers put up seem to always be big, square, blocky-looking things, and this design calls to mind those homes, so I hope it's also incredibly useful for the birds.

Once you're done and once your new birdhouse is up, head back inside with binoculars and maybe make some hot chocolate to enjoy the show. It's a memory neither of you will soon forget.

HERE'S WHAT YOU NEED

- ❏ 1 piece of 1" × 4" wood—long enough to cut 8 equal-sized rectangular blocks
- ❏ 1 scrap piece plywood—enough to provide base and roof
- ❏ Wood glue or glue gun
- ❏ Screws—nice deck screws to withstand the elements
- ❏ Wooden dowel—thin, like a perch; 1/8" works great
- ❏ Stain and/or paint
- ❏ Bird seed!

TOOLS

- ❏ Saw (handsaw works but power is better for this project)
- ❏ Drill
- ❏ Drill bits (1" bit for openings and 1/8" bit for dowels)
- ❏ Sandpaper
- ❏ Ruler or measuring tape

HERE'S WHAT YOU DO

1 The first thing you want to do is make wood blocks out of your long piece of 1" × 4". Yes, you can definitely use a 2" × 4", especially if you have one lying around, but I just like the lighter feel and look the 1" × 4" provides—it's less thick and clunky. It's up to you; either works fine. At any rate, measure out eight equal lengths on the strip. I used 8" lengths, but you can use pretty much anything you want. That said, I wouldn't go more than 10"—otherwise the house begins to take on some serious heft.

2 Once you have your blocks measured out, grab a saw and start cutting. You can use a handsaw, but try to find something more powerful if you can. It goes faster and the cuts are cleaner, especially as you near the last pieces and you're fed up with the handsaw.

3 Now you have eight equal-sized rectangular blocks. Build a house with them! Seriously, make a mockup. You can make the house in any design you want—with the two side pieces acting as bookends for the two front pieces, or the two front pieces acting as bookends for the two side pieces. I like the look this method provides: jamming the end of one piece into the side end area of another, and then repeating that all around. Once your house looks suitable for birds, sand all your pieces and make them as smooth and purty as you can on the outside. Keep the insides rough, otherwise you could quite possibly commit bird murder, as they need a rough surface to help them climb out. Birds are surprisingly picky. Have you ever seen those *House Hunters* episodes where the shoppers go around ragging on paint jobs and tile work? Birds make those people seem perfectly reasonable. Still, help them out a little, would you?

4 Once your blocks are good to go and you're happy with the layout of your house, it's time to start gluing. Slather some glue where the pieces will join up, being careful to wipe up any excess, because you'll be staining later and glue drips look weird under stain. During this process, imagine you're building a two-story house. Use four blocks to build the first floor, and then the other four blocks to build the second floor. You can definitely try to build a third floor, but I don't know why you'd want to, unless you're trying to catch a turkey, say, or an emu. When you're done building the two stories, glue them together and lay your scrap piece of plywood on top. Now put some weights or something heavy on top of the plywood. Let the whole thing dry.

(If you'd like, you can use a hot glue gun to speed up the process. Oooh, sacrilege! I can hear Bob Vila crying.)

5 Once dry, your house should be a perfect little box. Now grab your drill and make guide holes for your screws where each block joins another—two holes per joint. Once down, start screwing the pieces together. Make sure you get screws that will be able to withstand the elements, like deck screws or outdoor screws.

6 Your house is looking pretty awesome at this point and feeling sturdy. Put the whole thing on your plywood and trace out a floor. You can either make the floor match the house exactly, or you can add an extra 3" in the front to provide a "porch" for the birds. *(See Fig. 1)* There's no right way to do it. The porch effect just lets you sprinkle seeds on it to attract birds. If you don't actually *like* birds, of course, forget the porch. Now, cut out the floor and glue it

on. Add a couple of screws from the bottom to make it permanent. Also, drill a few small holes in the bottom for drainage. Again, birds = picky.

7 Before you forget, like some people I won't bother to mention, now is a good time to drill a hole for the birds, a front door so to speak. A 1" drill bit provides the perfect size for most small birds. Drill one hole, two, three, fifteen, however many you want—just make sure one is close to the floor, so they can climb out.

8 The roof is a little tricky, if you decide to go with the slant look. You could just cut out a piece of plywood to match the top of the house, screw it on, and *boom*, you're done. But if you like the look of the slant—I think it provides a sweet 1950s vibe to your yard—you'll have to build a dowel system. Think Ikea. Measure out a rectangle of plywood that will overhang just a little on the front and a lot on the

Fig. 1

Fig. 2

sides, so that the birds will be protected from wind and rain and hungry creatures. (Keep the roof flush to the back, so that you can later hang it on, say, a fence or a tree.) Cut it out and get ready to dowel.

9. Using a drill bit that matches the size of the dowel—again, ⅛" works perfectly for the dowels—drill two holes on each top side piece of your house. One hole should be located 2" from the back and another hole should be located 2" from the front. These will be your dowel holes.

10. Cut out four dowels. Two should 2", and two should be 3". Stick them in the house dowel holes. *(See Fig. 2)* Almost done. I swear.

11. Now you'll need to make dowel holes for the plywood roof. You can go the mathematical genius route and do all the measurements required to line things up properly, orrrrrr . . . you can do this: Insert the dowels into the house and put a dab of paint on each tip. Keeping the roof hovering above the dowels, eyeball it into place until you're happy with the look. Then gently lower it until you hit the painted tips of the dowels. You should have perfectly placed markings for where to drill your dowel holes on the roof now. Drill the holes at the tips, making sure not to go through the roof.

Secure the roof to the dowels but don't glue it yet. Just make sure everything fits into place and you're happy with the look. You can decrease the slant either by cutting the dowels shorter or drilling deeper into your house for the dowel holes (don't drill too deeply into the roof).

12. When you're happy with how everything looks, it's time to stain. You can paint the whole thing or stain the whole thing. Do anything you'd like. Personally, I like the look of a nice house stain to complement a bright painted roof.

13. Once everything is dry, before you glue the roof on, consider for a moment how you plan to hang the house and where you plan to put it. You can drill two more holes in the rear of the house and then screw the house onto a yard fence. After it's secure, glue the roof on (this is why your roof has to be flush with the rear of the house). Or, you can use plastic zip ties to secure the house to a tree if you like, before adding the roof. Use the drill holes in the rear of the house to pass the zip ties through and loop around the tree. Once happy with the location, glue up the dowels and then add the roof.

14. If you went the "front porch" route, sprinkle some seeds on the porch and then head inside with some binoculars and hot chocolate to enjoy your very own wild animal show!

FLYING SHIRT

If this didn't make me smile every time I think about it, I'd feel horrible about this craft.

My poor daughter was so let down. You should have seen her face.

We were walking downtown to meet her mother for lunch one day and somehow our conversation turned to flight. For summer vacation she wanted me to help her devise a way to fly.

Yes, fly. As in, "The flying kid of San Francisco." She had it all planned out.

We talked and talked about various wing contraptions and glider outfits until we finally settled on this: a flying shirt. We'd take an old T-shirt, cut it up, and insert some fabric for wings. Every time she raised her arms, the fabric between her side and her arms would pull tight and provide the lift needed for flight. Think flying squirrel.

I thought she had a better chance of growing *real* wings than getting any actual distance with this getup, but Emme was already too far gone, lost in the idea that it could really, truly work. On our walk, she started eyeballing the tall buildings, talking about how she would soon be able to leap from one to the other thanks to her flying shirt. She even suggested that on an upcoming road trip to her grammy's house she could soar above the freeway while my wife and I remained earthbound in the car below.

Her eyes shone with possibility and reminded me how much I love hanging out with this kid all day.

So it saddens me to think of her enormous letdown when we made the shirt during the break and then agreed to test it out from her bunk bed first before attempting a cross-state flight or leaping off any buildings. During the test, she made me back out of the way and hold open the bedroom door.

"Just in case I fly away," she earnestly explained. "I don't want to smack into it."

It was all I could do to keep from smiling.

On the count of three, she jumped off her bunk bed, stretched out her arms, felt the fabric go taut, and then slammed into the ground a split second later, her legs crumpling beneath her.

"Oh well," she sighed after a few more attempts, "It's still a pretty cool shirt."

Indeed.

HERE'S WHAT YOU NEED

❏ A long-sleeved T-shirt—Any of the kid's old T-shirts will do, just so long as you don't mind cutting it and sewing it back together.
❏ Fabric—about a yard of any solid color
❏ Sewing pins (lots!)

TOOLS

❏ Sewing machine
❏ Scissors
❏ Pinking shears (optional)

HERE'S WHAT YOU DO

1 Turn your T-shirt inside out and cut open the seam that stretches from the wrist to the hip. Just follow the seam and cut it out. You'll notice sometimes that the shirt rips in weird ways, and that's fine. You'll be sewing it together later.

2 Once the shirt is cut, lift the arm pieces so that they are at a 90-degree angle from the body, as if a kid had raised his arms straight out at shoulder height. Now, take your yard of fabric and cut out a square large enough to fill the space between the outstretched arm and the side of the shirt down to the hip. This fabric will be your wing on that side. Tuck one corner of your square into the armpit of the shirt, tucking it in about an inch into the shirt. Then stretch out the adjacent corner of the fabric to the wrist while again tucking about an inch of the fabric into the arm along the way. Do the same on the side until it looks like the shirt has eaten up two edges of your fabric square. Don't be afraid to manhandle the fabric to make it work.

3 Cut the fabric from the wrist to the hip until you have a nice rounded shape. Repeat steps 2 and 3 for the other arm wing.

4 At this point, you'll want to finish the rounded portion of your wing, as this part will be showing. The other, straight edges will be sewn into the shirt, so don't worry about those. For finishing, you have a whole bunch of options. You can simply cut it and leave it at that, although the fabric will likely fray during washes. You can use pinking shears, which cuts down on the fraying. Or you can fold over the edge a tiny bit and sew a line of thread through it. Up to you. The fraying can be useful in making the shirt more "bird like," while the sewing finish makes everything look cleaner and sharper, as if you bought it in a toy store.

5 Once you finish the edge on your rounded piece of fabric, it's time to start pinning. This part sucks. No two ways about. It takes patience and grit but the finished product is worth it. You're going to have to take all your wing fabric and fold it and tuck it *inside* your shirt, making sure that the edges match up to the edges of the cut part of your shirt, which should still be inside out. Once the fabric is inside and once your edges match, start pinning the pieces together. *(See Fig. 1)* Remember, you are smarter than fabric. It will bend to your will.

Pin one part and then move about an inch down the line and keep pinning. The more pins the merrier—you can sew right over them or pull them out when the sewing machine gets close to them. It's a good idea to put one or two pins at the armpit area and then start pinning from the wrist going into the pit. If you find you have extra fabric or it's just not going well, the armpit is a good place to conceal mistakes. You won't even notice really. Same goes for the side. Start at the hip and keep pinning, going up to the armpit. When you're finished, you should have a big sausage of fabric that looks like something out of a horror movie. Congrats. You did it!

DAD TIP

Here's an easier, alternative way. Turn your shirt back so that the right side—the part that shows to the world—is on the outside again. Now insert the wing fabric into the shirt again, with the sharp corner in the arm pit, the straight edges about an inch into your cut and the rounded part connecting the wrist to the hip. Once you're happy that everything is lined up, pin it together and sew from the wrist to the hip, closing your cut seam along the way and sealing your wing fabric into the shirt. At this point, you'll need to repeat this process with the other arm wing, and then go back with the scissors and cut off any extra shirt flaps to clean it up. *(See Fig. 2)* This is sooooo much easier than all that pinning. And honestly, kids won't care. Plus—and here's the bonus of this part—you're done! Now go have fun.

Fig. 1

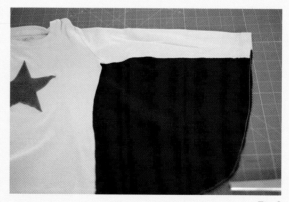

Fig. 2

6 Once your shirt sausage is ready to go, it's time to move on to the sewing machine. When you're sewing from the wrist to the hip, take extra care to sew only the edge. This process will reclose your seam cut and seal the fabric inside the shirt. Once you're done sewing, turn the shirt inside out and *boom*, out comes your wing. It should be locked in tight and appear to be part of the shirt, as if you just pulled it off a store rack. Again, take care when sewing, as the fabric bunches and you don't want to accidentally sew the arm closed or sew a line of thread through the wing inside. Repeat the pinning and sewing for the other arm wing and you're ready to fly. But please, don't jump off anything too tall. Because between you and me, *the shirt does not actually work for flight*. Your kid won't care, however. Have fun!

TERRARIUM

You know those people whose homes are just overflowing with plants? And I mean *perfect* plants: hanging plants, big, potted ones flowering in a corner, or little ones sitting primly on desks, like accomplices.

I am not one of those people.

I go to a plant nursery and can almost feel the tension as I walk by, as if the herbs and shrubs and perennials are secretly shooing me away.

"Please," they seem to say, "why don't you go to the lumber section instead?"

But hey, if you're in the mood to listen to someone who believes greenery speaks to him in fearful whispers, take this piece of advice: Go make a terrarium.

This is hands down one of my favorite projects, not only because you can probably re-use something you already have in the house for the container but because you don't have to go out and buy a boatload of necessities. Plus, if you forget to water it, a terrarium somehow survives—thrives even. And on top of all *that*, you get to dig your hands into the dirt and get messy.

I love it.

A simple hike or a trip to the backyard can probably provide most of what you need for a beautiful terrarium that will brighten up your living room or make an excellent gift or office decoration.

HERE'S WHAT YOU NEED

- ❏ Dirt
- ❏ A terrarium container (I used an old fishbowl, but a big vase or even a plastic Coke bottle will do.)
- ❏ Plants (If you have succulents or cacti in the yard, trim a few and use those—you don't need much!)
- ❏ Moss or lichen (Again, not much; a very, very small handful)
- ❏ Small rocks
- ❏ Small play figurines

HERE'S WHAT YOU DO

1 You need dirt. That's Job Number One. You can get fancy. You can go to your local nursery and buy perfect terrarium fertilizer and cactus soil and little batches of sand that would just look so perfect and quaint bundled together in a glass bowl. This is totally cool and worth it and makes for a nice terrarium all for around thirty bucks. Or you can just go dig a hole in your backyard and get most of those things for free. I've found that my most successful terrariums have had a mix of soil: regular dirt, some small rocks, sand, you name it.

2 Put the dirt mixture into the bottom of your container, layering it for design if you wish; for instance, rocks and sand on the bottom, soil on top. The rocks on the bottom help drain the soil and keep it nice, so by all means, feel free to start there. But don't fret if your little garden helper just wants to jam in a bunch of dirt. It will all work out but you'll just have to make sure you don't overwater in the future. No biggie.

3 Grab some plants you like and make a small design with them. For instance, you could make a "river" of rocks cutting across the scene, with small plants on one side and dirt or moss on the other. Just sprinkle some stones in a line and voilà, instant river. Maybe clump some plants or moss to the side. Maybe leave some soil visible. You can jam everything in or you can add just one or two plants here and there. Make a design first before you start planting the plants, so you know what you're aiming for.

4 Once you have a design in mind, start planting. You don't have to dig a ginormous hole in the terrarium and then fill everything in. Just use your fingers to push aside the dirt, add your plant, and use your fingers to fill it back in. *(See Fig. 1)* You can clump plants together or not. The really great thing about terrariums is that you can just pull out the plants and start

Fig. 1

over. Take your time. Let the kids do the planting. If it doesn't work, try again.

5 For a final touch, once everything is planted, insert a small toy figurine into the scene. For instance, one of our terrariums boasts a tiny pirate. Another holds a bird. Kids seem to delight in adding to the scene, as if they are creating a new and perfect world just for them.

DAD TIP

Two things: One; take your time. Go on some hikes to gather supplies. You don't need more than a small handful of plants. Although you can plant a terrarium in all of a half hour, it may take longer to gather your materials. Make it all part of the project and have fun. Two; watering a terrarium is super easy. Depending on your container, you may need to only sprinkle a cup of water a month into it. This can be a great early chore for kids old enough to start pulling their own weight.

DIY JACKSON POLLOCK

I'll always remember the look on my daughter's face the first time we did this.

The idea arose when I took her and my cousin to the San Francisco Museum of Modern Art, where we viewed a Jackson Pollock painting. It looked like someone had just poured paint all over a canvas.

"Please," my cousin sighed, "I could do that." She pointed at Emme. "Heck, *she* could do that."

At the time, Emme was three and into painting, and I wondered: *Could* she? Could *I*?

It was worth a try.

I converted a spare room into a makeshift art studio, covering the floor and the walls with plastic sheeting and newspaper. Once the room was reasonably protected from damage, I put a big piece of canvas on the floor, handed my daughter some paint and a stick, and said, "There's only one rule: You can't touch the canvas. Otherwise, go to town."

You should have seen her eyes. It was almost as if I handed her a can of paint and said, "Here, make the biggest mess you possibly can."

Wait. It was *exactly* like that.

In the end, it turned out Emme actually could do it. Her painting turned out so well that we hung it in the living room, where it remains to this day. I then tried—twice, in fact—and could never quite get it right. It turned out that the only people who can really do this well are Jackson Pollock and children.

I did some research on Jackson Pollock and how he painted. I'd recommend his way: doing it outside and using sticks or the pointy end of brushes to dip into the paint and then drip onto the canvas. He also used a lot of home wall paint. It's a lot more runny and drippy than your kids' tempera art paint or, say, acrylics. Otherwise, add a little water or paint oil to your craft paints to make them more pourable or drippy.

Mostly, though, just get out of the way. Put the canvas down and let the kid go for it.

HERE'S WHAT YOU NEED

- ❏ Tarp or plastic sheeting (if painting inside, buy a *lot* of plastic)
- ❏ Canvas—the bigger the better
- ❏ Paint—wall paint, or watered-down craft paint in three or four colors

TOOLS

- ❏ Sticks
- ❏ Brushes
- ❏ Sponge brushes (holds paint well)
- ❏ Whatever you want to use to drip paint

HERE'S WHAT YOU DO

1 Find a good space outside you won't mind getting a little or a lot paint-y. Spread your tarp out and then put your canvas on it. *(See Fig. 1)*

2 Open up your first color of paint, hand to child and, well, begin. You can do the no-brush rule if you want, as I think it lends a more authentic JP vibe to the whole thing. But do what you want. It ain't rocket science.

3 It's important to let the first color dry pretty well—or at least until it won't blend with the next paint—before you start with your second color. That is why this takes a weekend to finish. Pouring and dripping and flinging paint everywhere doesn't take all that long. Waiting for each coat to dry does. So plan accordingly; otherwise you will end up with a blobby, runny mess.

DAD TIP

This is an excellent project for letting the kid take charge all the way. I mean, it's not that complicated. You're tossing paint into the air. Find a space you're comfortable to get messy in and go for it. Just make sure you don't wear any clothes you'd like to wear to church later. Everyone is going to get messy.

That's pretty much it. Fling paint. Wait to dry. Fling more paint. Done!

Fig. 1

READING CHAIR

At the end of a long day, when I finally have a free moment—the kid is in bed, my wife is upstairs crafting, all the chores and school duties are done—I like nothing more than slipping into my reading chair with a good book. It's my space, a place to call my own.

I wondered one day: Wouldn't my child appreciate that same special space? Indeed she would.

This is a project that requires very few tools—none, in fact, so long as you can find the right chair. It requires simply sandpaper, some paint, and a few hours around town and around the house.

In the end, your child will have a special place to call his or her own for reading or lounging or just chilling out. This project is a great way to spend some quality time together as you search for a chair and work on a simple craft that will be sure to please for months, if not years, to come.

HERE'S WHAT YOU NEED

- ❏ A child's chair (one you're okay with painting)
- ❏ Sandpaper
- ❏ Paint—and brushes

TOOLS

- ❏ None at all, unless you find a chair that needs a screw or two here or there to make it sturdy

HERE'S WHAT YOU DO

1 Go on a treasure hunt. If you don't have a child-sized chair you're okay with sanding down and painting, spend a few hours trolling your city's thrift stores in search of a perfect-sized chair. This is half the fun of this project, as your kid will be in charge of the hunt and will be out there searching for the key ingredient for his or her own special reading space. In all likelihood, you'll find a perfectly beat-up old chair for $5 to $10 that will work out just fine. Have fun with this step and make a day of it. There are great lessons in here about turning someone else's discarded junk into another person's treasure.

2 Now that you have a chair in hand, break out your sand paper and get to work. *(See Fig. 1)* This is something that requires

more than a little elbow grease. Thankfully, the chair is probably super small, so it shouldn't take that long and it's a perfect opportunity for kids to take the lead. The idea is to remove any old paint or stain to get it ready for the next step: painting.

3 Speaking of which . . . it's painting time. You can do it one color that fits the decor of your house. *(See Fig. 2)* You can do it multicolors or design it some way to make it look less ghastly, less like a child . . . well, painted it. But why? This is not your reading chair. This is your kid's. Let him

Fig. 1

Fig. 2

or her sketch out some designs and then go to town, choosing everything from drawings to colors to whatever. *(See Fig. 3)* The idea is to create something special and unique for your child's tastes, so let the kid take the lead. Yes, younger kids will paint disasters that make even Thomas Kinkade paintings look appealing. But you'll be surprised at the awesome sauce older kids come up with.

4 The painting process may take an afternoon or it may take a few days. Once everything is dry, find a space in the house that will fit the chair just fine. Maybe near a bookshelf that's a special place just for the kid's books, so that when she's in her chair, she has instant access to her own world of imagination and leisure.

Every now and then, the house goes suddenly quiet—too quiet—and I peek out from the kitchen to find the kid in her chair, flipping through a book. That's the end game for this project. So have fun and let the kid take the lead.

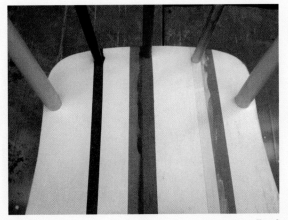

Fig. 3

FABRIC BANNERS

You never know what you'll need to throw a party. And fabric banners like these are the perfect accessory.

We like to hang these for birthdays. Imagine waking up on your special day to a house festooned with decorations in your honor. Now imagine you're six or ten or forty-two.

How flippin'awesome would *you* feel? Exactly.

The neat thing about making your own fabric banners is that they can be a living project—something you keep adding to over the years. You can use old shirts, pieces of beloved blankies, swatches from some special coat or toy, or whatever. Whenever you suddenly find yourself with special fabric you don't know what to do with or whether to even store, take a little time for a few snips and stitches to increase the length of your celebratory banner and create something not just festive but highly personal.

That's just one idea. You can use any fabric you want. This is a great project for leftover scrap fabric from other projects (flying shirt or cape, anyone?). You can even make a bunch of different banners for different holidays. Once you get the hang of it, you'll find yourself thinking more about fabric banners than you ever thought possible.

You're welcome.

HERE'S WHAT YOU NEED

❏ Fabric—at least eight 12" × 12" swatches to get started

❏ Bias tape (You can make your own, but I recommend buying ready-made for beginners.)

TOOLS

❏ Sewing machine

❏ Iron

❏ Scissors

❏ Pinking shears

❏ Pins

❏ Chalk

❏ Measuring tape (A construction tape measure works fine, but if you have a sewing machine, my guess is you also have a sewing tape or even a measured cutting surface.)

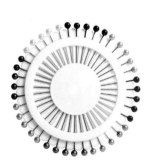

HERE'S WHAT YOU DO

1 Iron all the fabric to remove any creases or wrinkles. Now fold the swatch in half so that the pattern is showing on both sides. The "right" sides should be facing out, in other words.

2 Now it's time to measure. Your triangles should be 6" across at the base. They should then be about 8" long, going in toward the center to form a tip. Mark the dimensions with chalk on the folded fabric. (Yes, these sizes are arbitrary. You can make triangles any size you want, especially depending on how much fabric you have or who's doing the cutting. Just make sure you have one straight edge for tucking into the bias tape and a pointy end for dangling. I've also seen rectangle banners, so you can go that route, too. Again, arbitrary!)

3 Now you have a bunch of triangles measured out with the pattern showing on both sides. Take your pinking shears and cut out the triangles. *(See Fig. 1)*

4 Now pin the triangles together just as they are, so that they'll stay in place as you move to sewing. A few pins in the center of your triangles should hold the fabric together just fine. Now you're ready to sew.

5 Run a stitch from one edge of the triangle's base going down to the point then back up to the other side of your base. Try to stay close and even to your little pinking-shear cuts—say, no more than ¼" from the edge. Don't worry about stitching along the base, as you'll get to that in the next step.

Fig. 1

Fig. 2

6 Now the finishing part. Take your bias tape and open it up just once—you don't have to unfold it all the way. Just open the first fold so you have a really long "pocket." You're going to stuff the bases of the triangles in this long pocket and pin them in place. *(See Fig. 2)* How much space should you have between each triangle? Again, an arbitrary answer: five inches. But you can eyeball any distance you think looks perfect. Just make sure you pin the bases into the bias tape, because you'll want to stitch them in during the next step.

7 The bias tape should now be riddled with triangles just itching to be stitched into place. Well, go to the sewing machine and do it! Run one long row of stitches from one end of your bias tape to the other, being sure to stitch in each triangle base along the way. This process seals the triangles to your tape and also closes the bias tape "pocket" to provide a finished product.

8 Cut off all excess thread and *boom*, you're done. You can use simple push pins to hang your banner anywhere you want.

If you run across some special fabric you want to include, you can make your banner grow by continuing to add more triangles to different bias tape and then sewing that new tape onto the edge of the old. Pretty easy.

DAD TIP

If you decide to make your own bias tape using fabric you have on hand, I highly recommend using a bias tape maker—a small device that takes a long, rectangular strip of fabric and helps you fold it into the shape of bias tape while you iron. You can find these at your favorite craft or fabric store. Buy a 1" tape maker for a fabric banner.

SCHOOL BREAK

3

PROJECTS

BICYCLE JUMP

I'm including this one with a caveat. Someone you know and love just might break her teeth on it. So be careful.

Here's the backstory.

We neighborhood kids were messing around on our super-sweet and glittery banana-seat BMX bikes when one of us had the great idea to build a jump. We stacked some wood in the street, put some plywood on top of that and then spent the next thirty minutes in bike-riding nirvana before *someone* (I won't name names) went head over handlebars and smacked into a manhole cover, incisors first.

It probably would have been wiser to nail all that wood together.

But your kids are probably smarter than I was.

Bottom line: Kids are going to build ramps and jumps. There's no stopping them. So you might as well point them in the right direction.

This is a simple ramp structure you can teach them to build themselves. If it looks like something a kid built, well, it should. Because that's the point. The kids should be able to put a lot of this together themselves. I took out any angled cuts or newfangled scientific things, such as exact measurements, and more or less re-created those silly ramps we used to build as kids, but with the added bonus of screws and nails!

If you have older kids or are looking for something with more daring to it, you can very easily hack this jump design to provide for better lift and seemingly higher air. (The hack follows in the last step.)

HERE'S WHAT YOU NEED

- ❏ 2" × 4"s—four 8' lengths (You may not use all of it, but it's better to have more than less.)
- ❏ Plywood—a half sheet of 5-ply is ideal
- ❏ Screws—lots of 2½" deck screws

TOOLS

- ❏ Saw
- ❏ Drill
- ❏ Measuring tape

HERE'S WHAT YOU DO

1 Cut two 50-inch strips of 2" × 4" and lay them parallel to each other about 18" apart. This will be your base and help prevent the kind of teeth-rattling disasters that you might remember from makeshift childhood jumps.

2 Now cut eight 18"-long pieces of 2" × 4". You are going to lay these across your base.

3 Screw in one 18" piece at one end of your base, about 4" from the edge. Go to the other end of the base and repeat with another 18" piece. At this point, the base should be sturdy.

4 For this next part, it really depends on how high you want to make this jump or how much bike-riding skill your kids possess. If your kids are ready for something more daring, stack three of the 18"-long pieces of 2" × 4" across the base about 18" from the edge of your base. *(See Fig. 1)* Imagine you're going to soon lay some plywood on top of this business. If you're okay with that angle of jump, screw one piece to your base and then keep stacking and screwing in the pieces until firm. If your kid is only ready for a smaller jump, try stacking two 2" × 4"s at this point instead of three.

5 Repeat this process on the other side of the jump base, being sure to match however many 2" × 4"s you chose to stack in the middle. While you can't vary the height at each side, you can definitely vary the length. If you stack the middle 2" × 4"s about 18" from the edge of the base and on the other end, stack them about 24" from the edge. This provides for a longer, gentler ramp slope once you add the plywood.

Fig. 1

6 Once the 2" × 4" support pieces are screwed into place, it's time to work with the plywood. See how the base is 18" across? You want to cut all your plywood to match that, creating long, 18"-wide strips of plywood. *(See Fig. 2)*

7 Along with stacking and screwing in the wood, this next step is what makes this such an intuitive, kid-friendly project. Don't screw anything in yet. Just lay the plywood down on your ramp, running from the ground, over your single 2" × 4" and then up to the middle of your taller stack of 2" × 4"s. You don't have to be super exact. Just make sure you cut the plywood long enough that you can screw one edge at the middle of your tallest 2" × 4" stack and then overhang the base far enough to hit the street. (You don't want the end of the plywood to be too high off the street, otherwise your ramp will cause a sudden stop, as opposed to a cool jump.)

8 For the purposes of providing you with a better guide, here are the measurements of plywood for a fairly gentle ramp: 27" long going up from the street to the 2" × 4" stack located 18" from the edge of the base; and 37" long going from the street to the 2" × 4" stack located 24" from the other end of the base. See how there's an open middle spot now between two cool ramps? Measure that space and cut plywood to fit. Again, don't screw anything in yet. Just make sure the wood all fits.

9 When you're satisfied with how the plywood rests on the wood and how each plywood piece meets the other and how both end pieces meet the street, it's time to screw it all down. Please don't add screws in the middle of your plywood in the places you imagine someone might be riding a bike. Instead, add them on the sides, going into the 2" × 4"s below. *(See Fig. 3)* Two going into each 2" × 4" below should

Fig. 2

Fig. 3

be enough. Make sure to make them even with the plywood or even countersink them a tiny bit.

10 Now you have a ramp that goes up, levels off, and then goes down again. I've found that younger kids who are not quite jump-ready can use this as a ramp to get the feel for more action. Older kids can still catch air and then use the other side as a landing strip, or even try to clear the other side altogether.

11 If, however, your older kids, or particularly daring younger kids, want something more jump-y, you can take the same structure and cut off the base at the end of your tall stack of 2" × 4"s. After doing that, you still have the base of two 2" × 4"s running parallel and 18" apart from each other. You still have one piece of 2" × 4" spanning the base about 4" from the edge. And you still have a stack of three 2" × 4"s, but this time that stack is at the very end of your base. Lay a strip of plywood from the edge of the tall stack going down across your single piece and then into the street. Screw into place, and whammo: super-cool ramp.

DAD TIP

You can increase the height by adding length to your base 2" × 4"s and then adding more stacks of 2" × 4"s, but I wouldn't add any stacks higher than four pieces, as the structure might begin to get wobbly.

OL'-FASHIONED FRUIT CRATE SCOOTER

The idea for this one came when I saw one of those Facebook memes about how the "future portion" of *Back to the Future Part II* is almost upon us. The "future" arrives in 2015, in fact.

The movie promised us so much: hoverboards, flying cars, self-tying shoelaces. We only have a few years left, and I have a sense we're all going to be seriously let down.

That silly meme always gets me thinking of the future and the past. Remember the cool fruit crate scooter that Marty McFly hijacked and turned into a skateboard when he visited the 1950s? Well, if you can't make your own hoverboard, you can settle for one of these, and believe me, you won't be disappointed.

Okay, okay, fine. This is the twenty-first century. There are *hundreds* of scooters available. Toddler scooters, kid scooters, professional *adult* scooters. Why on *earth* would I want to build some relic from the 1950s?

Because it's *cool*. Because your kid will not only love building this thing but will love tooling around the sidewalks on it, decorating it, and stuffing toys or gear in it. Because you can do something really fun together and also provide a window into the nostalgic fun your child's *grandparents* had before even skateboards were thought up. Heck, this would be a perfect project for grandparents and kids.

And if all that's not enough, there's this: because you *can*.

I saw a replica scooter like this in a retro toy catalog going for about $150 and thought that was insane. The whole idea behind a fruit crate scooter is to use wood and spare parts from around the house to make your own fun. Take this project as a lesson in re-use and gumption, and then get ready to hit the road. You won't believe the reaction these creaky things get.

HERE'S WHAT YOU NEED

- ❏ Old skateboard (or just wheels and trucks if you have them)
- ❏ Old fruit crate (some craft stores sell cheap replicas if you can't find one)
- ❏ One 3' piece of 1" × 6" lumber
- ❏ One 2' piece of 1" × 4" (if needed for tall kids)
- ❏ One short piece of dowel or stick (for handlebars)
- ❏ Wood screws—lots (1½")
- ❏ Wood glue

TOOLS

- ❏ Saw
- ❏ Drill
- ❏ Measuring tape
- ❏ Pencil
- ❏ Pliers
- ❏ Screwdriver

HERE'S WHAT YOU DO

1 Take the trucks and wheels off an old skateboard. True, this is a cheat. Our grandparents used to build their own axle and wheel system for their scooters, attaching the whole shebang to the bottom of their lumber boards. Well, good for them. It's fun to take apart an unused skateboard for this, as the wheels roll nicely and the process is easier for kids to work with.

2 Put the crate on one edge of the 1" × 6" lumber, standing it vertically so that the opening of the crate is facing inward, where your little rider will stand. Make sure the edge of the crate is flush with the short edge of the board. See how the crate takes up about 10 or so inches of the board? Mark that with a line on the 1" × 6". From that line, you'll need an extra two feet or so to actually stand on. So measure out from your first line an extra two feet and cut your board there. *(See Fig. 1)*

3 Once you have a long scooter board—almost 3' in length—attach the skateboard trucks and wheels to it. *(See Fig. 2)* You can probably use the same small bolt and nuts that came with the skateboard. Score! Sand the board to make it smooth and ready to go. You can stain or paint

it later. (Take note of where skateboard wheels are located on skateboard and install trucks on your lumber to roughly match the layout.)

4 Now you have an almost-homemade skateboard. You can stop here if you'd like and mess around with the "new" board. Or you can go on to the next step: attaching the fruit crate. Put the crate back on the way you had it before, lining up the edge of the crate with the edge of the board, as well as the line you marked. Lift it up, add some glue where the crate will stand and then put in six small wood screws: three near where rider stands and then three where the edge of the crate meets the edge of the board. As for the size of the screws, you want them to go through the crate and into the board but all the way through the board.

5 At this point, you should have a fruit crate attached to a skateboard. Cool. Weird maybe. But cool. If your little rider is the perfect size for this height of scooter, screw in your wooden dowel or sanded stick going across the crate for handlebars and you're done. *(See Fig. 3)* Not too difficult, right? Well done! If your rider requires a little more height, go on to the next step.

For taller riders, take your 1" × 4" piece of lumber and put it on the board so that it is flush with the fruit crate and standing up vertically. Have your little rider stand right behind it and eye-ball what a good handlebar height might be. Cut the wood accordingly. *(See Fig. 4)*

Once you have the perfect height for handlebars, screw the 1" × 4" to the fruit crate at the top and bottom, using three screws going across. If you'd like, you can also screw a few from the bottom of the skateboard going up into your vertical 1" × 4", but be very, very careful that the screws don't emerge from the wood. Sharp points are not fun to stand on.

When the 1" × 4" is in place, add the wooden dowel to the top of it with a few screws. You can also use a sanded stick, as long as it's sturdy enough. *(See Fig. 5)* That is the last step. You are now the proud owner of a scooter that people won't be able to stop gaping at. Seriously, give it a whirl on the sidewalks and just watch as people—older people especially—say, "How cool!" or "I used to have one of those!" Fun times.

Fig. 1

Fig. 2

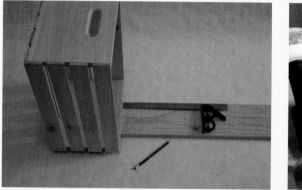

Fig. 3

Fig. 4

Fig. 5

SEESAW

Remember all that stuff I said about the joys of working together? About the beauty of re-using supplies you already have around the house? About really letting the kid take the lead?

Yeah . . . um . . .

Building a seesaw tests all that.

Or as my father-in-law likes to say, "Measure twice, cut once, curse a little bit, and then measure again."

I don't mean to scare you off. This may be one of the more involved projects in the book, but the payoff is *huge*. And honestly, it's really not *that* bad. There's just a lot of steps, but the basic theory is the same. Just throw a plank over a fulcrum and have fun.

If you're looking for a simpler way to have some good ol'-fashioned seesaw fun, I'm including an alternative version at the end of this chapter—a version that truly does require nothing more than a log and a plank of wood.

But if you're ready to move on with something that will absolutely flip your kid's lid when it's finished, this one is for you. In all honesty, you won't believe how much joy a simple seesaw will bring into your life, especially when you team up to make it.

HERE'S WHAT YOU NEED

- Two 8' lengths of 2" × 6"
- One 8' length of 1" × 6"
- Two roughly 1' pieces of 1" × 4" (for seats)
- Two dowel pieces (about 10" each, for handles)
- Three 8' lengths of 2" × 4"
- One 10" bolt, ¾" diameter, threaded all the way through
- Two ¾" nuts
- Two ¾" washers
- Box of deck screws (one box of 2½" and one box of 3½" long)
- Wood glue

TOOLS

- Circular saw
- Drill (including ¾" drill bit and a bit to match dowel size)
- Measuring tape
- Combination T-square
- Sandpaper (lots!)
- Pencil
- Vices or clamps, gumption, thesaurus of child-friendly curse words

HERE'S WHAT YOU DO

1 You can divide this project into two basic parts: the see and the saw, or the plank you ride and the fulcrum it rests on. It doesn't matter which piece you start with, but to get going, let's start with the plank.

2 For the plank, you'll need the two 8' lengths of 2" × 6" and the 8' section of 1" × 6". Pretend you're making a giant wooden cookie. The 2" × 6"s will be the outside, and the 1" × 6" will be the filling. Mmmm, cookie.

3 The good news is you don't need to cut the outside of the cookie—the 2" × 6"s—as they are already a good length at 8'. But you do need to sand them really well, as kids will be grabbing all over them, even with handlebars. Make sure they're smooth.

4 Now you can move on to the filling, or the 1" × 6" piece. You'll need to cut this into three sections—one 3' length and two 16" lengths. The 3' section will go in the middle of your cookie. The smaller sections will go exactly one foot from each end, standing vertically and perpendicular to your plank, to provide a place for handles. The bottoms of each 1" × 6" piece of filling should be flush with the bottoms of your cookies.

5 You can decorate this stuff any way you want. Turn those 16" lengths into miniature zebras, using a jigsaw for carving and then some paint. You don't have to use any special pattern. Draw what looks interesting and go from there. You can use any design you want or you can leave the pieces as is. Please note, however, that you might want to do something with the sharp corners. Either give them a serious sanding to round them off or, even better, cut off the tips and then sand. No matter which design you choose, use a drill bit that corresponds to your dowel size and drill one hole in the middle of each piece. The placement doesn't have to be exact—just in the middle and toward the top or wherever you think your kid might hold them comfortably. **Note**: Don't install the dowels yet!

6 Now that your filling is ready, you're ready to start gluing and screwing. Put one side of the cookie (2" × 6") down and then glue your filling to it, with the longer piece in the middle and your future handlebar pieces one foot from each end. You should have enough room to sit on the edges of the 2" × 6"s and be able to reach your handles. Don't worry about any gaps between the pieces, as this thing will soon be as sturdy as a brick house. Now glue the top of the cookie onto the filling. Your sandwich should look complete. But before you start screwing it all together, make sure the bottoms are flush and the pieces are where you want them to be. If you have clamps or vices, install them now. Even if you don't use them this should turn out just fine, especially if your little helper keeps thing straight and even.

7   Now for the fun part. Add four screws to the middle of the plank, being sure to go through the filling and into the cookie on the bottom (3½" screws). Then add two screws to each end area, again being sure to go into the filling and bottom cookie. During this process, make sure the end pieces don't shift around and become uneven.

8   Once you're done screwing in one side, flip it over. It should be pretty sturdy at this point, but let's clamp this sucker down. Again, add four screws in the middle and two for each end piece. Please be careful not to screw in the same locations where you already have screws coming from the other side. There's lots of room on the wood to play with. Figure it out.

9   Once it's screwed in, your plank should be sturdy as all get-out. Now it's time to add seats. Take your pieces of 1" × 4", sand

them ridiculously well, and then fit them onto the ends so that they are flush with the handlebar wood (the vertical filling). The seat can overhang the ends a few inches if you'd like. *(See Fig. 1)* Not too much, however; 12"- to 14"-long seats work perfectly. Lay the seat flat across the wooden plank and add at least four screws, drilling down into the seat and through the 2" × 6"s below. Rescrew any screws that poke through. This is key, as little dangling legs will be playing in this area and sharp points aren't fun. Congrats! Your plank is now done . . . almost. But the big drilling needs to wait until the fulcrum is complete.

10 Now it's time to tackle the fulcrum. For the fulcrum parts, you're basically going to build two short A-frames and then cross-brace them at the bottom and top before running a vertical piece across the braces. The ¾" bolt will run through those vertical braces, and then through

Fig. 1

your riding plank. That's the short story. Here's the long story on how to get there.

11 Take your 2" × 4"s and get ready to cut. You'll need a table saw to cut at 45-degree angles, or you can break out your combination T-square (a great tool!) to mark 45-degree angles before cutting with a circular saw. *(See Fig. 2)* Again, I'd highly recommend borrowing a power saw of some kind, as you'll do a lot of precision cutting on this one and a handsaw sucks for it. Use the best you have or can borrow.

12 Form an A-frame by cutting two 36" lengths of 2" × 4" with 45-degree angles on each end. Match up the angled pieces to form an A. **Note:** The top of the 2" × 4" should be angled to form a tip, while the bottoms should be angled to form flat footrests once the A shape is made. Pencil this out first on wood before cutting. *(See Fig. 3)*

13 Now you need to brace these A's. Measure up four inches from the bottom of your A legs. Lay across a piece of 2" × 4" and mark your 45-degree cutting lines. This is how long the bottom brace will be (43½"). Cut the 2" × 4" at 45-degree angles to match the angle of the A legs and then glue and screw them into place. Your A should now be feeling pretty sturdy. Almost done.

14 Now you need a brace at the top. Measure 1½" down from the tip of the A. Lay across a 2" × 4" piece (short) and mark the angle to match the slope of the A-frame. The longest points of your 2" × 4" should be about 10". Cut at angles to match the angle of the A legs and then glue and screw them into place.

15 Once the A has two braces going across it—at the very top and the bottom—you're going to add one final piece of 2" × 4". It will run vertically from the top edge of the

Fig. 2

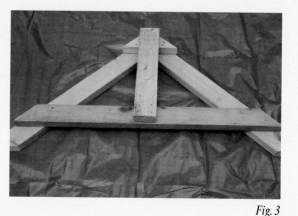

Fig. 3

top brace to the bottom edge of the bottom brace (20½"). Glue and screw this into place. This piece will bear the weight of your riding plank and riders, so go ahead and screw the bejesus out of it, or more technically, put four screws into each brace.

16 Repeat this A-frame construction until you have a matching pair. Your plank will go between them.

17 At this point, find the very middle of your plank and mark it clearly. It's important to find the very middle, as you want the weight of each side distributed equally.

18 On each of the A-frames, measure down 5" from the top of the vertical braces and mark that point clearly in the middle of the vertical braces. This is where you'll be drilling holes. Make sure the hole will be lower than the top 2" × 4" cross brace and then mark this section clearly on each A-frame.

19 Once everything is measured, lay one A-frame down so that your vertical brace is facing up. Lay your plank across it so that the very middle part is directly over the spot you measured on the vertical brace. Now lay your other A-frame down so that the vertical brace hits the plank. You've basically created another cookie, with the A-frames acting as the outside this time and the plank acting as the filling. **Note**: It's very important to get the middle piece of the plank lined up with the middle of the vertical braces. Once you're good, use vices or clamps to lock that all down.

20 Now you can break out the ¾" drill bit and drill a hole through the top vertical brace, down through the plank and then through the bottom A-frame vertical brace. Take your time. Do it as straight as possible. This is where the ¾" bolt will eventually go.

21 Speaking of which . . . once your hole is drilled, run the bolt through a washer and then all the way through the hole, adding a washer and a nut on the other side. Don't go crazy on the tightness just yet. Just test it out and see how it all works. See how the plank goes up and down, up and down? You are *so* close.

22 Take a look at the top of your A-frame now. It's pointy. It doesn't really influence the action of the device, but it does provide a potentially dangerous eye-poker. If you're okay with that, I admire your coolness under spousal fire. If you're not okay with it, take a handsaw to the tip or unbolt the A-frame, remove the plank, and then cut the tips off the A, giving each A-frame a flat surface on the top.

23 At this point, you can reassemble your seesaw, tightening the nut on the bolt and then adding a second nut behind that for extra security.

24 To add more stability to your seesaw, you should now add more braces. If you've got really young, light kids, you don't have to worry about that right away if you want to play for a bit. But you'll need to add them eventually as the kids get older and more vigorous in their play, or if you plan on doing some seesaw action yourself. As you'll see in the next two steps, it's really pretty simple.

25 When you're ready to add the braces, just cut a 2" × 4" to lay across the top of the A-frames, resting on the tops you just cut off to improve safety. Screw it down into place. (I thank my father-in-law for this ingenious design, which not only prevents serious eye damage but also helps brace the whole system.)

26 While you're at it, measure out two more braces that will stretch from one A-frame to the other. Be sure to install these toward the bottom of the A's, because if you put them too high, the plank will hit them during play.

27 Once it's sturdy, break out your paint or stain. If you paint, make sure you choose

an exterior house paint or an exterior weather stain, as this thing will be outside in the elements.

DAD TIP

If there's one piece of advice I would offer about this project, it's this: Take your time. There's a lot of precision cutting involved and a lot of screwing-in and drilling. If your helper is really young, make this a longer project. If your helper is older, you can get this done in a weekend. Just be prepared for a lot of steps and a lot of cutting and drilling.

Okay, *now* you're done. Have fun with it!

Seesaw alternative

Let's say you have a log or have access to a log. Let's also say you have a long piece of 2" × 6". Simply lay the 2" × 6" across the log, roughly in the middle of your plank, and voilà, insta-seesaw! You can devise a system using dowels to hold the plank on the wood better, but why bother? Your kids will be having too much fun to care.

Yes, it's that easy. It's not perfect by any means. But it really does work in a pinch.

BACKYARD SWING SET

My friend Graham inspired this swing set with his own backyard version. It's a very simple design and relatively easy to build but please, take note, you're going to need some help—very likely more help than your little helper or helpers are able to provide.

My father-in-law, daughter, and I tinkered with some different designs and bracing strategies, and every now and then we'd have to call out for even *more* help.

So make this a longer project that involves a good friend with a strong back. The kids can put together the swings and help with all the drilling and assembling. But at various points along the way, you're going to need a strong hand for lifting.

I'm giving you two versions for getting this done. Both require the exact same amount and sizes of wood. The bolts are the same, although the second version requires fewer of them. The only real difference is the hardware you use to connect the A-frame bases of the swing set to the top crossbeam.

After playing with Graham's set and then building our own at home, I recommend going the full store-bought route and buying what's called the EZ Frame Bracket and Brace system. It's slightly more expensive ($8 for each bracket instead of $5 or so for my hardware hack), but I found the premade brackets much easier to work with and more secure feeling than the ones my father-in-law and I created with stuff from the hardware store. No matter which version you choose, I'd recommend still using the EZ Frame Braces (different from brackets) because they are so secure and easy to use.

You can save money by making your own system to connect the swings to the swing set, as opposed to buying expensive, ready-made kits. I used a $30 heavy-duty system to connect one swing and then built my own hardware hack version for a fraction of the cost. I recommend the hack version for this part of the construction because it's cheaper and appears to be just as safe. In fact, I was so annoyed at the cost of the more expensive version that I'm not even including it as an option, but you can find those things online pretty easily.

HERE'S WHAT YOU NEED

VERSION ONE (RECOMMENDED)	VERSION TWO

WOOD

- ❏ Four 4" × 4"s—8' long
- ❏ One 4" × 6"—10' long
- ❏ Two 2" × 4"s—8' long

WOOD

- ❏ Four 4" × 4"s—8' long
- ❏ One 4" × 6"—10' long
- ❏ Two 2" × 4"s—8' long

HARDWARE

- ❏ EZ Frame Brace—four total
- ❏ EZ Frame Bracket—four total
- ❏ Fourteen $\frac{5}{16}$" carriage bolts, $4\frac{1}{2}$" long (galvanized steel)
- ❏ Fourteen $\frac{5}{16}$" washers (galvanized)
- ❏ Fourteen $\frac{5}{16}$" lock nuts
- ❏ Drill bit—$\frac{5}{16}$" diameter (see tool notes at the end of the materials list for the swing)
- ❏ Wood screws—3" long

HARDWARE

- ❏ EZ Frame Brace—four total
- ❏ Simpson Strong-Ties—four total
- ❏ Twelve $\frac{5}{16}$" carriage bolts, $4\frac{1}{2}$" long (galvanized steel)
- ❏ Twelve $\frac{5}{16}$" washers (galvanized)
- ❏ Twelve $\frac{5}{16}$" lock nuts
- ❏ Drill bit—$\frac{5}{16}$" diameter (see tool notes below)
- ❏ Wood screws—3" long

HERE'S WHAT YOU NEED
THE SWING

WOOD
- ❏ One 1" × 6"—18" long

HARDWARE
- ❏ Two ¼" eyebolts
- ❏ 4 ¼" washers
- ❏ 2 ¼" lock washers
- ❏ 2 ¼" lock nuts
- ❏ 2 ¼" regular nuts
- ❏ 4 sturdy carabiners
- ❏ 6'–7' of metal chain, 500-pound weight (you can always tie up any extra)

WHAT YOU NEED FOR THE SWING CONNECTORS ON THE BEAM:
- ❏ 4 eyebolts—each ½" diameter and 7" long
- ❏ 4 really big washers—½" diameter
- ❏ 4 lock washers—½" diameter
- ❏ 4 lock nuts—½" diameter
- ❏ 4 sturdy and slim carabiners

TOOLS
- ❏ Drill with *great* batteries
- ❏ Saw
- ❏ Combination T-square
- ❏ Measuring tape
- ❏ Special tools—multiple long drill bits: one ⁵⁄₁₆" drill bit, at least 7" long; one ½" drill bit, at least 7" long; one ¼" drill bit

HERE'S WHAT YOU DO

1 Let's start by creating A-frames with the 4" × 4"s. You should be able to get 8' lengths from the hardware store, which is great because you won't have to cut them. Lay them on the ground so that the inside edges of the tips touch on one end. The other ends should open up to form an A shape. The layout should be almost a perfect isosceles triangle, with 8' on each side and 8' in the long gap between the open ends.

2 If you bought the EZ Frame Brackets for Version One, directions are, thankfully, included in that pack. But it's also very intuitive. You line up the bracket at the tip of the A-frame and insert the screws in the pre-drilled holes, making sure the top is level to support a beam on top later. *(See Fig. 1)* Pretty easy really.

3 If you're going with Version Two, you'll have to buy Simpson Strong-Ties—shiny metal bracket pieces. They are also pre-drilled, but we were never able to find them with 90-degree angles to support this design. You'll have to bend them yourself into a roughly 90-degree angle (place between two big pieces of wood to brace them and then push the slots down), so that you can screw the side into the 4" × 4"s and then be able to rest a beam on top in the slots. *(See Fig. 2)* (Again, the EZ Frame Bracket is premade for this. It makes the project much easier, especially if you're working with kids.)

4 Whichever product you choose, you'll have to repeat this drilling process on both sides of the 4" × 4" tips, so that you use four brackets total on your two A-frames.

Fig. 1

Fig. 2

5 Now it's time to switch to the beam before you lift it on top of the A-frame base. I'm not offering a hack for this one, as the EZ Frame Brace system is really sturdy and cheap. Plus, drill holes are marked out for you. And on top of all that, there are specific instructions included in that pack. (Follow the instructions on the pack, but be sure to install all your brackets to the beam *before* you lift it into place. You'll be using your ⁵⁄₁₆" drill bit and then six of the ⁵⁄₁₆" carriage bolts for this part.)

6 After you install the braces to the beam, you're not quite done with the beam. You'll want to install your hardware to hold up the chains and your swings. Make sure you measure a good distance from the edge of your beam—30" works great. Mark that spot. You will install one eyebolt here. From that spot, measure in toward the center of the beam 17". Mark

that spot. You will install another eyebolt here. These two bolts will hold one swing.

7 To install bolts, take your ½"-diameter drill bit and drill through the beam. Top to bottom, bottom to top. It doesn't matter. Just make sure it's as straight as humanly possibly.

8 This next step is key. When your beam is finally lifted and in place, you will want the eye in the eyebolt to be facing *down*, toward the ground. Install accordingly by first adding a big washer to the bolt and then going into your beam from the *bottom to the top*—again, so the eye faces the ground when the beam is in final place. *(See Fig. 3)* Once you twist or hammer in the eyebolt, put on the biggest washer, then the lock washer, and then your lock nut. Secure it all in place and repeat at your next mark 17" away.

Fig. 3

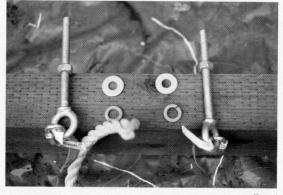

Fig. 4

9 At this point, you should have two eye-bolts ready to attach a chain to. *(See Fig. 4)* Sweet. Nice job. Measure out a safe distance to where you want your next swing to be. A two-foot gap between swings should work perfectly. Repeat the eyebolt process starting there and giving yourself 17" of space between each new eyebolt.

10 Once your eyebolts are installed, you're ready to lift the beam. This is where help will definitely come in handy. In fact, this is where help is necessary. My friend Graham did this part by himself and almost *died*. Okay, not really. But I can imagine *I* would have died. The point is, get help. It's easier.

11 With both versions it's pretty intuitive. You lift the beam onto your A-frame and then start screwing in and drilling where all the holes tell you to screw and drill. Before screwing in the beam, lock down the other ends of the four EZ Braces to your 4" × 4"s. Drill in screws first and then break out your $5/16$" drill bit to make holes for your $5/16$" carriage bolts, just like you did to install them to the beam.

12 Once your braces are in place on the 4" × 4"s, you can move on to the brackets. For the EZ Frame Brackets, you'll need to drill $5/16$" holes for more carriage bolts on each end. Drill in screws first to secure it and then drill holes for bolts. After that, add the carriage bolts as directed.

13 For Version Two, simply add screws in all the places the brackets show you can add them.

14 At this point, you are mostly locked down and good to go. Your A-frame should feel sturdy and the beam should be in place and also sturdy.

15 To make it even *more* sturdy, you should cross-brace your A-frame by cutting a 2" × 4" to turn each A into a triangle. The lower you go, the more sturdy. **Note**: If you end up adding two cross braces to each A, which you can do for added stability, please be aware that you just created an instant ladder that every kid who sees it will want to climb. If you're okay with that, make sure you use a lot of screws. If not, one cross brace is enough.

16 To prevent wobble and leg lift—or even tipping—you can buy anchors, which you attach to each leg and then sink into the ground once your swing set is where you want it to be. This is a good idea but not needed right away if you have very small kids. Older kids and adults can get the set rocking, however. The anchors are readily available online.

 17 For the swings themselves . . . look, you can just buy some plastic versions. But wooden swings look cooler, along with the fact that you can make them yourself with some scraps of wood and simple hardware.

Fig. 5

18 To make a swing, take your piece of 1" × 4" wood that is 18"-long. *(See Fig. 5)* Lop off each corner. Sand like crazy all around, as you'll have butts and legs and hands all over this thing.

19 Once it's nice and smooth, measure in 1" from the middle of the side and drill a hole using your ¼" bit. Repeat on the other side.

20 Now install your ¼" eyebolts by first installing a washer and a regular nut on the bolt before running it through the wood. On the other side of the wood, install a regular washer, a lock washer, and a lock nut and then tighten. Repeat on the other side. *(See Fig. 6)*

Fig. 6

Fig. 7

21 To attach the chain to the swing, you'll need your four carabiners for each swing: two small ones to connect the chain to the seat bolts and two bigger ones to connect the chain to the eyebolts at the beam. *(See Fig. 7)*

22 You can make two swings repeating this process. Or you can mix it up. It's *your* swing set, after all. I also like to have some rope on hand for more freeform climbing or swinging. Really, with some chain, some rope, and some carabiners, there's no limit to the kind of devices you can add: rings, trapeze bars. Emme and I are working on one of those rocking horse swing deals.

So there you go. You just built a swing. You are a backyard rockstar. I mean it. That is a difficult project—or at least one that involves a lot of steps and a lot of lifting. With the brackets and braces, it's really intuitive and takes the thinking out of it, for the most part. But it's still a project that takes a lot of time. I hope you'll enjoy your hard work!

Acknowledgments

Unheralded legions of people go into each and every book (well, not physically—I hope). From those who provide inspiration and encouragement to those who provide editing, research help or, if you're really lucky, butt kicking, there is much work behind the scenes.

I'd like to especially thank Jeremy Adam Smith for helping to get this project started; the entire, beloved online community at the *San Francisco Chronicle's* parenting blog *The Poop* (including its amazing editor and my friend, Peter Hartlaub); my own amazing community at Cry It Out!; and each and every teacher and newspaper editor I've ever had. I can still hear you screaming: "Hurry!" "Wake up!"

Many people were key in helping to bring this book together, including my amazing agent, Mollie Glick, and Katie Hamblin at Foundry. I owe particular thanks to my editor, Ross Weisman, for not killing me with each and every stupid question. I have never met editor Peter Archer and copyeditor Kate Petrella, but they did an amazing job of correcting all my errors without making me feel dumb. It is a gift.

On a more personal level, I am indebted to my mom, Teena Adamick, for ingraining the idea of re-use with each and every trip to the thrift stores, and to my brother, Tom, for providing a lifetime model of hard work and perseverance. I am also insanely grateful for my in-laws (how often do you hear that?) not only for the artistic inspiration (looking at you, Marilyn Farley) and not only for helping with some of the very projects in this book but for patiently teaching me so many fundamentals of home construction over the years (thank you, Duane Kromm!).

Mostly, I am forever grateful to have met and married the most inspirational and supportive woman I have ever known, my wife, Dana Kromm. She is my craft partner in crime and my guide for how to live life to the fullest. I lerve you.

And Emmeline, none of this would be possible without you. I think we make a pretty good team, you and I, and I'm so glad we have the opportunity to share our adventures so that other families can feel the same joy you provide us with each day. Thank you!

STANDARD U.S./METRIC
MEASUREMENT CONVERSIONS

VOLUME CONVERSIONS	
U.S. Volume Measure	**Metric Equivalent**
⅛ teaspoon	0.5 milliliter
¼ teaspoon	1 milliliter
½ teaspoon	2 milliliters
1 teaspoon	5 milliliters
½ tablespoon	/ milliliters
1 tablespoon (3 teaspoons)	15 milliliters
2 tablespoons (1 fluid ounce)	30 milliliters
¼ cup (4 tablespoons)	60 milliliters
⅓ cup	90 milliliters
½ cup (4 fluid ounces)	125 milliliters
⅔ cup	160 milliliters
¾ cup (6 fluid ounces)	180 milliliters
1 cup (16 tablespoons)	250 milliliters
1 pint (2 cups)	500 milliliters
1 quart (4 cups)	1 liter (about)
1 gallon	3.8 liters

WEIGHT CONVERSIONS	
U.S. Weight Measure	**Metric Equivalent**
½ ounce	15 grams
1 ounce	30 grams
2 ounces	60 grams
3 ounces	85 grams
¼ pound (4 ounces)	115 grams
½ pound (8 ounces)	225 grams
¾ pound (12 ounces)	340 grams
1 pound (16 ounces)	454 grams

OVEN TEMPERATURE CONVERSIONS

Degrees Fahrenheit	Degrees Celsius
120 degrees F	49 degrees C
140 degrees F	60 degrees C
200 degrees F	95 degrees C
250 degrees F	120 degrees C
275 degrees F	135 degrees C
300 degrees F	150 degrees C
325 degrees F	160 degrees C
350 degrees F	180 degrees C
375 degrees F	190 degrees C
400 degrees F	205 degrees C
425 degrees F	220 degrees C
450 degrees F	230 degrees C

LENGTH

U.S.	Metric
1 inch	2.54 cm
1 foot	30.48 cm

BAKING PAN SIZES

U.S.	Metric
8 × 1½ inch round baking pan	20 × 4 cm cake tin
9 × 1½ inch round baking pan	23 × 3.5 cm cake tin
11 × 7 × 1½ inch baking pan	28 × 18 × 4 cm baking tin
13 × 9 × 2 inch baking pan	30 × 20 × 5 cm baking tin
2 quart rectangular baking dish	30 × 20 × 3 cm baking tin
15 × 10 × 2 inch baking pan	30 × 25 × 2 cm baking tin (Swiss roll tin)
9 inch pie plate	22 × 4 or 23 × 4 cm pie plate
7 or 8 inch springform pan	18 or 20 cm springform or loose bottom cake tin
9 × 5 × 3 inch loaf pan	23 × 13 × 7 cm or 2 lb narrow loaf or pate tin
1½ quart casserole	1.5 liter casserole
2 quart casserole	2 liter casserole

INDEX

Note: Page numbers in *italics* indicate projects.